the Adaptive Teacher

Faith-Based Strategies to Reach and Teach Learners with Disabilities

JOHN E. BARONE ✦ CHARLEEN KATRA

LOYOLAPRESS.

LOYOLA PRESS.
A JESUIT MINISTRY

3441 N. Ashland Avenue
Chicago, Illinois 60657
(800) 621-1008
www.loyolapress.com

Unless otherwise noted, the Scripture quotations contained herein are from the *New Revised Standard Version Bible: Catholic Edition,* copyright © 1993 and 1989 by the Division of Christian Education of the National Council of the Churches of Christ in the U.S.A. Used by permission. All rights reserved.

The Sensory Experience Chart on page 39 is adapted from Brenda Smith Myles, *Asperger Syndrome and Sensory Issues: Practical Solutions for Making Sense of the World* (Shawnee Mission, KS: Autism Asperger Publishing Company). Reprinted with permission.

The Church Documents list on page 168 is adapted from Donna Toliver Grimes, *All God's People: Effective Catechesis in a Diverse Church* (Chicago: Loyola Press, 2017). Reprinted with permission.

The People-First Language Guide, Getting to Know Me Worksheet, Sensory Considerations Parent Questionnaire, and Visual Schedule on pages 169, 170, 174, and 179 are adapted from the *Adaptive Finding God* Program (Chicago: Loyola Press, 2015). Reprinted with permission.

Interior and cover design by Loyola Press

Illustrations by Jannie Ho and Loyola Press, except **17** Kathryn Seckman-Kirsch; **35**(bg) lasagnaforone/Getty Images; **38, 53** DrAfter123/Getty Images; **103**(bg)Thodoris_Tibilis/Getty Images; **179** Warling Studios/Karen Wolcott/Loyola Press.

ISBN-13: 978-0-8294-4516-9
Library of Congress Control Number: 2019942886

Printed in the United States of America.
19 20 21 22 23 24 25 26 27 28 Bang 11 10 9 8 7 6 5 4 3 2 1

To my parents, Anthony and Rose Iannucci, whose selfless and unconditional love always brought gospel values to life. Your legacy continues to inspire me.

—Charleen Katra

To my good friend Eugene Webb (1940–2018), whose wit and wisdom still serve as a constant source of inspiration in everything I write.

—John E. Barone

Contents

Welcome v

Foreword vi

Meet Your Guides viii

Introduction ix

CHAPTER 1: We Are All Reflections of God's Love 1

CHAPTER 2: Creating a Warm and Welcoming Learning Environment 11

CHAPTER 3: Recommended Learning Accommodations 23

CHAPTER 4: Integrating Sensory Supports into Your Teaching 35

CHAPTER 5: Promoting Executive Function and Self-Regulation 51

CHAPTER 6: How to Get and Keep Attention 65

CHAPTER 7: Effective Classroom Communication 79

CHAPTER 8: Peace Be with You: Managing Meltdowns 91

CHAPTER 9: Courtesy Can Be Kryptonite 103

CHAPTER 10: Becoming Lifelong Learners: No Stickers Required 113

CHAPTER 11: Can You Relate: Building Connections with Learners 123

CHAPTER 12: The Ghosts of Pedagogy Past: Forming Your Teaching Style . . . 137

CHAPTER 13: Viewing Disabilities as Differences 151

Conclusion 161

Common Diagnoses Glossary 163

Additional Resources 165
   How Inclusive Is Your Parish? 166
   Inclusive Learning Environment 167
   Church Documents on Disabilities 168
   People-First Language Guide 169
   Getting to Know Me Worksheet 170
   Saints for People with Disabilities 171
   Participant Information Form 172
   Sensory Considerations Parent Questionnaire 174
   I Can Pause Before Answering 177
   Visual Feelings Dictionary 178
   Visual Schedule 179
   Recommended Resources 180

WELCOME

In 2016, two experts in the field of catechesis for learners with disabilities set out to create a practical, easy-to-use guide to help teachers, catechists, and parish leaders effectively pass on the faith to all God's children. Their resulting hard work, imbued with warmth and wit, supplies novices and veterans alike with the encouragement and confidence needed to minister to children with disabilities as well as all typically developing children. This editor is proud to work alongside a talented duo who live out the book's mission every day in their roles as teachers of and advocates for individuals with disabilities in our Catholic faith communities.

In the following pages, you'll find a wealth of information organized around common areas of management for teachers, catechists, and parish leaders with the goal to help you

- create a warm and welcoming learning environment.
- better understand learners and their processing abilities.
- respond to learners' sensory needs.
- nurture learners' gifts and talents.
- best communicate with your learners.
- effectively gain and retain attention in the classroom.
- build your learners' listening and conversation skills.
- help all learners discover the richness of our faith and celebrate the sacraments.

The book was written in tandem by Charleen Katra, Associate Director for the Archdiocese of Galveston-Houston's Office of Evangelization and Catechesis, and John E. Barone, Director of the Learning Resource Center at Strake Jesuit College Preparatory in Houston, Texas. The chapters alternate between the authors' unique voices and styles as each covers an area of expertise. Charleen and John also weigh in on one another's ideas throughout, offering more tips and content reinforcement that add to the book's rich conversation.

Some of their practical tips, strategies, and activities that you can implement in various educational settings include

- engaging activities tailor-made for learners with disabilities as well as all learners.
- teacher tips for best practices.
- scripts educators can apply to common situations and issues they may face.
- conversation "chat bubbles" in which the authors add to one another's chapters.
- questions to help readers reflect on their personal experience and discern how to adapt or enhance their teaching style.
- notes section at the end of every chapter for professional development workshops.
- extended bonus materials, including blackline masters, charts, and reproducibles.
- tools and insights that parents of children with disabilities can use at home.
- guidance in helping learners become more self-aware and take more ownership of their strengths and disabilities.

While further training is always recommended in working with learners with disabilities, *The Adaptive Teacher* will give you the encouragement and support needed to successfully minister to individuals who need our help the most. In the following pages, we invite you into a discovery process of grace and awareness as you expand your knowledge, refine your practices, and offer meaningful catechesis and accompaniment for all learners.

FOREWORD

Think back to the first time you felt called to be a catechist or a teacher. For me, it was during my freshman year of college. I was living away from home for the first time, and one of the first things I did was find the Catholic student center. One Sunday in August, I saw an announcement in the bulletin there about a need for catechists at a local parish. Four of us signed up, and from then on, I began to teach a seventh-grade Confirmation class every Sunday morning as an eighteen-year-old student!

My mind went back to that experience as I prepared to write this Foreword. I imagine that many of you are catechists who are interested in finding ways to better communicate with your students. Others may be Catholic school teachers, parents, aunts and uncles, brothers and sisters—persons who are committed to a more inclusive learning environment for the good of all children and adults. What motivated you and brought you to this moment?

Charleen Katra and John E. Barone, the authors of this book, have motivated me personally and taught me a great deal about positive ways to communicate the beautiful news of the love of Jesus and the truth of the Catholic faith. I emphasize *positive ways,* as both authors have consistently presented practical ways to become better teachers to me and other learners. They have been catalysts for more effective teaching methods and classroom management for more than forty years. Reading their book reminded me of my original motivations and current hopes.

If we look back to our own motivation for becoming a catechist, teacher, or parish leader, each of us will discover something unique and special about our story. Whether we were reading a parish bulletin, discerning possible career choices, or answering a phone call, we felt a deeper purpose and call to teach the faith. Somewhere in the midst of our *yes* dwells the acceptance that God has created us, and we can pray with Psalm 139, "You knit me together in my mother's womb." This underlying acceptance of God's love may still be hard to express or even understand, yet I am convinced more than ever that God's love is the foundation of our motivation to teach the faith.

From this experience of God, we will begin to appreciate that all creation proclaims the glory of God, a beautiful thought that has practical applications. In a statement urging us to consider the most pressing needs of the modern world, the leaders of the Second Vatican Council wrote,

> Coming down to practical and particularly urgent consequences, this council lays stress on reverence for man; everyone must consider his every neighbor without exception as another self, taking into account first of all His life and the means necessary to living it with dignity, so as not to imitate the rich man who had no concern for the poor man Lazarus. *(Gaudium et spes 27)*

The challenge and call to create a culture that acknowledges every life as a gift from God to be treasured continues today. *The Adaptive Teacher* responds to that call, and it's what most excites me about this resource and the hope it offers. As I've visited with students and teachers in our schools and catechetical programs across our rural diocese, I've experienced great reasons for hope. Communities are committed to working together to create a learning environment as broad as possible. *The Adaptive Teacher* offers practical advice and steps drawn from personal experience that can help with this effort.

At the same time, there are currents in the world that we must acknowledge and face. Archbishop José Luis Escobar Alas of San Salvador published a prophetic *Pastoral Letter on the Feast of Blessed Oscar Romero* (March 24, 2016). In this letter, he analyzes the violence so prevalent in his society, and with spiritual and theological insight identifies the root causes of violence. Toward the conclusion, in paragraph 143, he writes, "The fight against violence is synonymous with fighting the root causes behind it: social exclusion, idolatry of money, impunity and individualism."

The first root cause of violence that he mentions is social exclusion. Archbishop José may be writing about the larger context of current El Salvador, yet the spiritual insight can be applied to our culture and our classrooms as well. A strong way to fight violence is to fight social exclusion—to make a place for all.

May God bless you, your families, your students, and your communities with a deeper knowledge of His love and a greater ability to communicate the message to every person in the world in which we live.

—Most Reverend Brendan J. Cahill, STD
Bishop of Victoria in Texas

Meet Your Guides

CHARLEEN KATRA is an Associate Director for the Archdiocese of Galveston-Houston's Office of Evangelization and Catechesis. She has been responsible for the Ministry with Persons with Disabilities for over twenty years. Charleen previously provided systematic and sacramental catechesis for individuals with intellectual and developmental disabilities at her parish. She currently serves on the Board of Directors for the National Catholic Partnership on Disability.

Charleen has a bachelor of science in Special Education and Elementary Education from Kent State University and a master's in Pastoral Studies from the University of St. Thomas in Houston. She speaks nationally on best practices for the successful inclusion of diverse learners: from faith formation and sacramental preparation to liturgies and parish life. Charleen believes that hospitality and evangelization are the foundations of this ministry which underscore Catholic social teaching regarding the dignity of the person. She is the author of *How to Talk to Children about People with Disabilities.*

© John Katra

JOHN E. BARONE is the Director of the Learning Resource Center at Strake Jesuit College Preparatory and the Executive Director of the DeBusk Enrichment Center for Academically Talented Scholars. He has extensive background in child and adolescent development, education, youth ministry, and teaching students with neurological differences.

John received his bachelor's degree in Religious Education from the University of St. Thomas in Houston and his master's degree in Private School Administration at the Institute for Catholic Educational Leadership, University of San Francisco. He is an accomplished workshop presenter, offering national workshops and teacher training. John is also the author of *A Place for All: Ministry for Youth with Special Needs* and *Jesus the Christ: Catechist Guide.*

© Genesis Photographers

Introduction

Hi, John! How are you?

Hey, Charleen! I'm great. What's up?

I just wanted to say that I am so excited to write this book with you and that it will be published by Loyola Press, a front-runner in this ministry. Our book will help shine a light on the great work that so many people are doing to welcome and include people with disabilities.

Yeah, me too! My hope is that it will encourage even more people to join in this cause. So much of what we have both been passionate about for years will go into this book.

Yes! Readers will discover the Catholic Church's foundation for ministry with persons with disabilities, which is based on our social-justice teachings and gospel values of inclusion.

Exactly. Many people are unaware of how strongly the leaders of the Church have been promoting inclusion. And for how long.

Did you know that November of 2018 marked forty years since the United States Conference of Catholic Bishops wrote their initial Pastoral Statement on People with Disabilities?

That was a long time ago! That's why it's so exciting to share this message with a larger audience. I've met many catechists who are terrified at the prospect of working with someone who has a disability. I think this book will help them be more effective, welcoming, and inclusive.

You bet it will. We can offer practical strategies that new and experienced catechists will be able to use.

☺ Absolutely! Let's also discuss old-school teaching styles vs. new, inclusive models and how to best adapt your own style to meet the needs of diverse learners.

Yes! I think all of us prefer being affirmed and feeling loved amid our learning. So, let's plan to talk about finding a balance between the two styles. Another important aspect we can explore is how to talk about and describe people with disabilities.

Can you believe there are still people saying things like "He's retarded"? Most of the time, I don't think people who use inappropriate terms are trying to be mean; it's what they were brought up with. So, let's include info on People-First Language, because words matter. ☺

Yes, and let's offer some tools for easing everyone's stress levels too!!

Amen! Why don't we divide the chapters up by areas we're individually strong in?

Same with how people manage a classroom—they tap into what they know. We should include some alternative classroom-management strategies, like replacing "Shhh!" with better attention-gathering methods. And we can teach when not to say *please* and *thank you* too.

Yes! Readers will notice that, much like teaching and learning styles vary from person to person, we'll each communicate the same message but write about it in different ways.

Yeah, courtesy can be Kryptonite to a catechist, and readers will discover why in this book. Let's not forget to add the two questions a catechist or teacher should never ask. . . .

I completely agree. Our writing benefits from our conversations about the material, since at times one of our perspectives may not include the same info as another.

Agreed, so let's plan to add the benefit of our thoughts to each other's work throughout the book.

Those are the best to know! Another super-helpful part of the book could highlight the benefits of having soothers and fidgets available to aid folks with sensory-processing disorders, which can make a world of difference for the individual and help avoid meltdowns.

Right. Our input will read like text messages—just like this conversation. I'll chime in with my comments, and you'll do the same. This will enrich the material.

Agreed! Well, I gotta run. Blessings!!

Kids screaming can scare the bejesus out of teachers, so information on how to work with learners who have a hard time controlling their emotions would prove ultra helpful.

You bet. Thanks for sharing in this adventure. Onward!

CHAPTER 1

We Are All Reflections of God's Love

BY CHARLEEN KATRA

Getting Started

As catechists, educators, parish leaders, or parents, we are called to a daunting but rewarding responsibility: to pass on the faith. To help us in this mission, God gives us each unique gifts to share with those we serve.

Whether we are veterans or beginners, our best response to the mission that God has entrusted to us is to gain a better understanding of the people we serve. In this chapter, we hope to enrich your understanding of children and adults with disabilities and the best ways to teach, reach, and pass on the faith to them.

Serving diverse learners requires additional training and great love. When we become more knowledgeable and sensitive to the experiences of others, we will find our own hearts responsive and magnified in turn.

TWO-MINUTE CHECK-IN

- How were you called to your ministry?

- What people, experiences, or invitations drew you to this vocation? How have they nourished you?

- How has this ministry changed the direction of your life? What challenges and rewards has it brought you?

SEEING PERSONS WITH DISABILITIES THROUGH GOD'S EYES

Persons with disabilities are authentically who God intended them to be, each person a reflection of God's love and grace in our midst. We need only open our hearts and minds—and the doors of the church and the hearts of the people inside—to receive God's blessings. For when we embrace our own authenticity and that of our sisters and brothers, we in turn praise and thank God.

In 2018, the Centers for Disease Control and Prevention reported that about 26 percent of adults in the U.S. have a physical, intellectual, emotional, or behavioral disability. It stands to reason that the same could be said for nearly every parish faith community. However, for a variety of reasons, people with disabilities are underrepresented in most churches. And while every Catholic has a baptismal right to be educated in the faith and prepared to celebrate the sacraments, persons with disabilities are still underrepresented in faith-formation programs and parish life.

The United States Conference of Catholic Bishops (usccb.org) and the National Catholic Partnership on Disability (ncpd.org) websites are great places to search for documents and resources for this ministry!

Thanks for sharing those, John. Big fan of both! 😊

ENCOUNTERING OTHERS AS JESUS DID

Our gospel values call us to welcome and include all persons, especially those who are marginalized and vulnerable. The Gospels are filled with instances of Jesus encountering people who had disabilities. He intentionally chose to spend time with them, to be in their homes and to break bread with them. Jesus modeled the love it takes to look beyond a person's disability and truly see the whole person, to get to know him or her and understand his or her hopes and dreams and fears. Jesus also shows us the empathy it takes to recognize ourselves in the other person, for we all have disabilities, some visible, some invisible; we all have strengths and weaknesses. We are more alike than we are different.

Did You Know?

Currently, about 26 percent of adults in the U.S. have a physical, intellectual, emotional, or behavioral disability.

WHAT IS YOUR ROLE IN INCLUSION?

So, what's a parish to do? How can a parish catechetical leader, catechist, teacher, or parishioner create the conditions for more intentional Christlike encounters? The more that individuals and faith communities learn about various disabilities, the more likely it is that their attitudes of acceptance will increase. The disability ministry is one of radical hospitality and true evangelization. Engaging in this ministry is an ongoing process that calls forth the gifts of every Catholic to be included so that everyone is blessed by being together and the Body of Christ is complete—love in action.

Thankfully, Jesus, the master catechist, has provided us with all the lessons we need to welcome, appreciate, and love others. For, when we open a door for someone using a wheelchair or act as a direct support for someone who has difficulty staying focused in class, we naturally promote opportunities for conversion in our faith communities. Is this not every parish's goal? In all aspects of inclusion efforts, from those who arrange and provide necessary support for others to those who witness how challenges are overcome through such collaborative efforts, everyone benefits and grows spiritually.

ALL CAN GIVE WITNESS

We each possess a spiritual life that needs care and nurturing. Faith-formation efforts can support and enhance the spiritual lives of persons with disabilities by seeing such individuals through the eyes of Christ and welcoming them into the full life of the Church. The *National Directory for Catechesis* states, "All persons with disabilities have the capacity to proclaim the Gospel and to be living witnesses to its truth within the community of faith and offer valuable gifts. Their involvement enriches every aspect of Church life" (*NDC,* #49). Every parish desires conversion for its parishioners. A person with a disability can preach the gospel to others in ways that some individuals in full-time ministry cannot! Many would agree that a parish needs the presence of persons with disabilities more than the other way around. By their very lives, persons with disabilities have lessons to teach us, if we are willing to slow down long enough to reflect on their giftedness.

All Christians are sent into the world to teach others about God. Some travel great distances to serve God's people. But it's not the distance that's important. By our Baptism, we are all missionaries, and we need only go as far as the next person God puts in front of us to spread his love. Christians who are growing in their faith continually strive to develop their knowledge, understanding, and behaviors to be more Christlike. The phrase "To hear the thoughts of one's heart, listen to the words that are spoken from one's mouth" may sound familiar. We know that spoken language evolves over time for a variety of reasons. One reason it evolves is to offer a more accurate and sensitive description of a human condition or circumstance—a naming of the authentic self.

CASE IN POINT: A PERSON FIRST

Many years ago, I attended a national disability-ministry conference. The opening session consisted of four panelists, who shared how they had experienced life with a disability. The last panelist to speak was Henry. He explained how he acquired a physical disability twenty-five years ago while working as a supervisor in a machine shop. He was in his mid-twenties at the time. On the day of the accident, an employee told Henry that a machine wasn't working properly. Henry took the place of the employee and began to inspect the machine, which was used to cut steel. Suddenly, the machine malfunctioned and cut off both his forearms. As horrible as the accident was to hear about, it was what Henry said next that caught my attention. He referred to himself as a "gimp."

The following morning, I happened to attend the same learning session as Henry. At the end of it, I mentioned to Henry that though he had referred to himself as a "gimp," I would never use that word to describe him. He proceeded to tell me about his journey with a disability as it relates to the way language changes over time. When his injury occurred twenty-five years ago, "gimp" was common jargon for someone without limbs and for other types of losses or limitations. Five years later, Henry was referred to as "crippled," a word that comes from the verb "creep." Another five years passed, and he was known as "handicapped." Five years after that, the term "disabled" was used to describe him. It's been five years since I met Henry, and the preference was, and still is, to use words that focus on the individual person (his or her name, if known, or gender) before stating any descriptor or diagnosis. This currently renders Henry as a "person with a disability," or more specifically, Henry, a man who has no forearms. This type of speech is known as People-First Language. Such language represents more respectful, accurate communication, and it acknowledges that there is much more to a human being than any disability or diagnosis. As for Henry, his self-identification with older terminology stems (not uncommonly) from the language used at the time of his injury.

Using People-First Language

To better understand the concept of People-First Language, let's consider an average traffic report. Turn on a television or radio in cities during rush hour and you will likely hear a live traffic report. For drivers trying to navigate their way to and from various locations, this is very helpful, particularly for finding out about traffic jams. Notice how these reports often begin with words like "There's a disabled vehicle on the northbound freeway. . . ." What does the word *disabled* mean to the listener in that context? It likely indicates that the vehicle is "broken down," "in the way," "not working," or a variety of other negative connotations. Hence, listeners will attempt to avoid this "problem." The use of the word *disabled* in describing an inanimate object, such as a vehicle, is perfectly acceptable. But from a Catholic-Christian perspective, we are challenged to move beyond using this word and other outdated terminology to using People-First Language.

> This is so true! Derogatory names and labels deny one's identity, authenticity, and humanity. No one wants to be put in a box!

As Catholics who believe and promote the social teachings of the Church, the first of which is the "Dignity of the Human Person," we are called to use only respectful language for human beings, all of whom are made in the image and likeness of God (Genesis 1:27). People-First Language always puts the person before any description or diagnosis. So, we don't say someone is "autistic" but rather that "a person has autism" or "a diagnosis of autism." And a person injured in an accident is "a person with a disability," not a "disabled person." In this way, we remove labels that hurt and reinforce negative beliefs, and we also communicate that someone has a disability or a diagnosis of a disability rather than referring to them as their disability or diagnosis.

> Labeling can sometimes be a reason that parents don't disclose a diagnosis. Or worse, parents may not agree on whether to disclose, causing an additional challenge to their marriage. Pastoral care and empathy are so very needed here!

A note of caution: How a person with a disability chooses to self-identify is a personal choice for the individual alone to make. Pastorally, we are called to respect his or her decision. As evidenced by Henry's story, one's choice of vocabulary may be closely associated with the terminology that was used when he or she was injured or diagnosed. Our goal is to improve the respect shown to people with disabilities by the words we use, while considering how one self-identifies.

Allowing for self-identification is important. Correcting people with a disability by telling them to call themselves something different defeats the purpose of showing them respect!

COMMONLY USED TERMS IN THE DISABILITY COMMUNITY

As in many fields, the need for a common language will often develop. For those of us who have responded to God's call to serve persons with disabilities, the following are brief definitions of disability-related jargon that you may begin to hear and find helpful.

We can avoid unintentional harm when we take time to listen to and respect the wishes of the people we serve.

Anxiety—An uneasy feeling that can result in symptoms of increased muscle tension, heart rate, and physical movement.

Buddy—A peer or older volunteer who assists an individual by acting as a companion to him or her and helping improve his or her engagement in activities and events. Buddies may also coach, tutor, or assist as needed.

Manic—A term used to describe a person who exhibits frenzied, exhilarated, or ecstatic behaviors that last for a significant amount of time. The person is likely to be energetic and need little sleep. He or she may be talkative and/or argumentative, enthused about any number of plans, many of them unrealistic. The person may be impatient or impulsive and resist any attempts to dissuade him or her from irrational plans or dangerous or harmful behavior.

Meltdown—An observable reaction by someone who is overwhelmed by stimulation from the environment, tasks, sensory input, people, or emotions, frequently resulting in a loss of self-control exhibited by screaming, aggression, panic attacks, running away, or intense withdrawal.

Nonverbal communication—Alternative ways a person communicates, often expressed through gestures, tantrums, pointing, leading someone to a door, etc. Electronic communication devices, picture boards, and the Picture Exchange Communication System (PECS)® are also included in this definition.

Nonverbal social cues—Communicating information through smiles, frowns, facial expressions, or body positions, without the use of words.

Panic attack—A serious episode of anxiety in which an individual experiences nausea, dizziness, palpitations, and/or shaking that are not due to medical reasons.

Picture symbols—Images that are used instead of words to provide information to someone who does not understand words.

Section "504"—A law from the Rehabilitation Act of 1973 that prohibits discrimination against individuals with disabilities. The law ensures that a child with a disability has equal access to education and that his or her needs are met as adequately as the needs of children without disabilities are. The child may also receive accommodations and modifications.

Stimming or stims—Self-stimulation, such as flapping one's hands or rocking back and forth in an effort to self-regulate or self-soothe.

> Sometimes I want to shout, "STOP STARING AT THE STIMMING!"

> There's a better way, John. 😳 People just need to understand that stimming is a coping mechanism used by persons with autism to try to self-regulate or calm down when overwhelmed by strong emotions or sensory overload. It's similar to how many of us may pace, click an ink pen, or shake a leg in response to an anxious feeling.

SUPPORTING FAMILIES OF CHILDREN WITH DISABILITIES

As Catholics, we need to remember that persons with disabilities and their families need our prayers and support. The United States Conference of Catholic Bishops states that, "often families are not prepared for the birth of a child with a disability or the development of impairments. Our pastoral response is to become informed about disabilities and to offer ongoing support to the family and welcome to the child" (*Welcome and Justice for Persons with Disabilities: A Framework of Access and Inclusion,* A Statement of the United States Catholic Bishops, #9). Any family with a member who has a disability can experience deep isolation within their faith community. When we open our hearts to one person with a disability, we open our hearts to the entire family, affirming their Catholic identity.

The very fact that God puts certain people in our lives is a sign that God wants us to do something for them. When we serve with a loving presence, we strengthen our relationship with God. This service not only reflects our hearts but also affirms every person, especially those with disabilities, assuring them of their human dignity and of Christ's love. Pope Francis, in *Evangelii Gaudium,* beautifully states, "Before all else, the Gospel invites us to respond to the God of love who saves us, to see God in others and to go forth from ourselves to seek the good of others." May we do so with great love and enthusiasm!

Pro Tip: SIGNAGE

As improvements to parish properties occur, signage should also be updated to indicate that parking spaces, building entrances, and restrooms are "accessible," replacing the words "disabled" or "handicapped" whenever possible. Signage can also be updated by displaying an icon of a wheelchair, a universal symbol of accessibility, in lieu of words.

Three Takeaways

- When we view persons with disabilities through the eyes of God, we will see that we are more alike than different.

- We are called to use People-First Language, which sees the whole person and respects everyone's inherent dignity.

- Our gospel values also call us to open our hearts and minds to families of children with disabilities, to support their faith journey and affirm their Catholic identity.

LOOKING AHEAD...

◆ Is mentioning a disability or a diagnosis even necessary in a conversation about a person with a disability? When is it appropriate to mention? When do you feel it's inappropriate?

◆ Imagine you're sharing the importance of People-First Language at a gathering of parents. One parent rolls his eyes and says, "This is just more politically correct nonsense. I agree you shouldn't call someone 'retarded,' but what difference does it make if I say 'autistic kid' instead of 'kid with autism'? People need to lighten up and not be so sensitive." How would you respond?

◆ What words would you want or not want used if someone were describing you or your loved one?

NOTES:

CHAPTER 2
Creating a Warm and Welcoming Learning Environment

BY CHARLEEN KATRA

Getting Started

Have you ever attended a class, a conference, or a party where no one greeted you or made you feel welcomed? You probably still remember that experience today. Chances are high that if you received an invitation to return, you probably wouldn't. No one likes to feel as though he or she is invisible.

Now imagine if that scenario had occurred differently. When you arrived, you were greeted with a smile, a handshake, a warm welcome, and an introduction to someone you didn't know. What a difference that arrival would make for you! In this scenario, would you return if invited again? Absolutely! Because when you feel seen by and known to others, you remember the experience fondly, as a blessing. How can we make sure our students feel just as warmly welcomed in the classroom, creating positive memories?

TWO-MINUTE CHECK-IN

- Is your classroom, church, or home warm and welcoming? What factors make it inviting?

- How do you welcome those who enter your space?

- In the past, who or what has made you feel welcomed when you've stepped into a new space?

COME TO THE TABLE

Think back to the last time you invited guests over to share a meal. You likely spent time deciding what food you wanted to serve and prepared your shopping list accordingly. You made sure the house was cleaned. You may also have taken extra care to decorate your table with candles, place mats, and fancier dishes. The time you put into creating a warm and welcoming atmosphere required intentionality. It didn't happen by accident.

Time spent at the table sharing a meal with others often reflects important moments in our lives. Many of us may look back on these times fondly, remembering the celebrations, conversations, laughter, prayers, security, and comfort. We may also remember feeling known and loved by those around us. In these moments, we knew we had a place—there may have even been a certain chair reserved for you. You were nourished at this table. You may have experienced a sense that everyone was cared for in individualized ways: The youngest may have sat in a high chair to fully participate; the second youngest could have been seated in a booster chair and near an older sibling or an adult; others may have been seated where they could easily serve and clear the table. No matter the seat, at this table, there was always an abundance of love and respect. Everyone mattered equally to one another. We may no longer remember specific words or conversations in detail, but the memories made from a warm and welcoming atmosphere are what linger in our hearts!

The table metaphor also symbolizes our faith lives: We all hunger. We all need to be nourished physically and spiritually. God invites everyone to come to his table and receive the bread of life. In our role as educators, we welcome everyone to the table, making space for all to receive God's invitation.

CULTIVATING A MINISTRY OF PRESENCE

Whether we're at the table or elsewhere, we all have the power to make others feel visible, known, and loved. Cultivating a "ministry of presence" in our interactions with others says to those around us, *I see you. I am present with you at this time and place, because God has ordained this meeting. I am grateful for this experience and bless you, in return, with my attention.*

As creatures of the Creator, we acknowledge that we are all made in God's image. For Catholics, that image is Trinitarian. Our belief in the Trinity is manifested in an understanding of our innate need to be in relationships—first and foremost with God and then with one another. For, whatever we call our closest relationships—a community, network, team, or family—the truth is we all need them!

Best Practices for Creating a Welcoming Learning Environment

We are given opportunities every day to make individuals feel not only visible but also valued. How can we ensure that everyone who encounters us for the first time or over countless times will feel both seen and appreciated? We start by having an attitude that aims to receive and treat everyone in the same warm, friendly, and generous way. Though our attitude and intent to be hospitable is foundational, the following are some best practices for creating a warm and welcoming learning environment:

- **Be prepared.** This will allow time to greet students as they arrive, which you can do by standing at the entrance to the room.

- **Offer your undivided attention.** Being attentive to each person and maintaining eye contact is an invaluable ministry of presence.

- **Be energetic.** An upbeat attitude sets a positive tone of excitement.

- **Personalize your greetings.** Students always enjoy hearing their names. (It's important to learn how to say and spell names correctly.)

- **High-five students.** High-fiving is a non-verbal way to engage someone upon arrival. You could also fist bump or shake students' hands. Be careful to always offer these physical interactions as an option, not a requirement, to accommodate those who are uncomfortable with touch.

- **Verbally identify yourself to a person who is blind or has vision loss.** Invite others to do the same.

- **Show genuine interest in every learner.** Incorporate a "Getting to Know Me" sheet to learn more, which can be found on page 170 at the end of this book.

- **Maintain a high level of patience and acceptance.** Offer a calm presence.

- **See each learner as a unique individual with valuable gifts to share.**

- **Be a strong proponent for bully-free environments.** Try hanging a sign that says "Our classroom is a place where . . ." and invite the class to complete it together. Afterward, make copies for learners to sign. In the process, you could discuss bullying behaviors, empathy-building activities, and healthy ways to respond to strong feelings, and then brainstorm acts of kindness that classmates can perform for one another.

- **Offer the same care and concern for every learner.** Honor the innate dignity of each person.

- **Extend personal invitations to parents/guardians to participate.** They can do so as a visitor, a guest speaker, or an aide.

- **Continue to learn.** Deepen your understanding of various learning differences and share what you learn with others in the process. Further resources can be found at the end of this chapter.

- **Identify youth or adults willing to be buddies.** A "buddy" can accompany someone needing extra assistance, which helps form relationships and lowers anxiety levels.

- **Simplify the environment.** Decluttering your space makes for fewer stimulations and a better learning environment for many. We will offer more tips for decluttering in chapter 4.

- **Teach everyone how to say "hello" and "welcome" in American Sign Language (ASL) or in another language used by one or more learners in the group.** You can find links to videos on how to do so at the end of this chapter.

- **Maintain calm.** Exhale, say a prayer, a sacred word, count to ten, whatever works best for you to proceed calmly.

- **Respond peacefully to situations.** We offer strategies on how to do so in chapter 8.

- **Encourage learners to use their gifts to serve God.** Call out their specific gifts whenever possible.

- **Support the development of every learner's potential.** Cultivating an interest in our learners' skills will help boost their self-confidence and desire to learn.

> At first glance, greeting students may seem like a small thing, but it's of tremendous importance! Especially for people with disabilities, who often arrive with a history of having been ignored, avoided, or stared at. This hospitality is nothing short of Christ among us!

> Exactly. Great lessons only improve when learners feel engaged and valued before teaching begins! Great things happen in the small moments of life, sometimes more meaningfully than in the big ones!

BUILDING STRONG RELATIONSHIPS

The famous theologian Henri Nouwen once said that "the teaching relationship is the most important factor in the ministry of teaching." What does that relationship look like? What if we could hear the unspoken thoughts of a teacher to appreciate this dynamic or, better yet, the thoughts of two teachers? If one were to demonstrate the teaching relationship at its worst and the other at its best, it would look something like this.

Teacher A	Teacher B
I'm in charge. You'll do what I say.	This is our class. We are all responsible for the learning that does or does not happen.
I speak; you listen.	I speak; you listen. You speak; I listen. We all have the right to speak, and when one of us speaks, everyone else listens.
You will win my respect by performing and behaving well.	You will have my respect regardless of your ability and behavior.
I'm always right.	Sometimes I can be wrong.

From those few examples, we can quickly get a sense of two polar models of teaching. Teacher A exemplifies a dictator model that intimidates and likely suppresses creativity and learning. Teacher B offers a mutual-respect model that promotes and encourages collaborative learning. The two exemplify the difference between "teaching versus reaching," or imparting knowledge versus connecting with students and inviting them into the learning process. Taking an occasional self-assessment of your own teaching style is always beneficial. Incorporating new ideas and positive behaviors can help you consistently offer your best to those you teach.

TEACHING IN A SHARED SPACE

First impressions do make an impact—and typically a lasting one. The first impression you make is essential, but the initial impression your learning environment makes is equally important. Oftentimes, the parish and school may share space. This can make managing the environment with others more challenging. But never underestimate the value of cultivating a positive relationship with those you're sharing space with. Here are a few tips to help you navigate sharing.

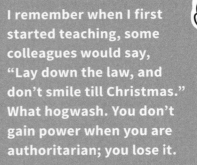

I remember when I first started teaching, some colleagues would say, "Lay down the law, and don't smile till Christmas." What hogwash. You don't gain power when you are authoritarian; you lose it.

Another benefit of the respect-centered model you describe is that you have fewer power struggles. A demanding "do-it-my-way" style will be met with resistance. Nobody likes being bossed around. And those with disabilities that include rigidity are more likely to respond to such demands with upset and refusal.

Or worse, a meltdown! Shifting teaching styles does take practice, and "best practices" are called "best" for a reason.

- Instead of feeling stressed by a need or an issue about seating arrangements or wall decorations, reach out to your counterpart and have an in-person conversation, if possible.

- Express gratitude for the availability of the space being shared.

- Respectfully defer to the person who uses the room the majority of the time.

- Ask for guidance or assistance in making any room changes between the different gatherings of learners.

- Remember that being visible and known to one another builds stronger bridges toward effective collaboration.

The more pleasant the atmosphere—from both the educator and the room—the more comfortable the learners will feel upon arrival and during their stay.

ASSIGNING SEATS

You may be tempted to allow students to choose their own seats when they first arrive in the classroom, as it gives them an opportunity to make a choice. Open seating is generally a positive and recommended practice. But when learners choose their own seats, the following may happen: First, they will probably sit next to friends or those they know and like, which does not create opportunities for new relationships and friendships. Second, students who are saving seats for friends may tell others to sit elsewhere—which would not feel warm and welcoming. We would never want anyone to have such an experience if we could prevent it from happening.

Saint Holy Cards Activity

Considering the above scenario and knowing that we want to promote the development of new relationships, here's an idea for you to try. The Church is well-known for having a long history of beautiful rituals and strong traditions. Some learners with intellectual or developmental disabilities or learners on the autism spectrum highly enjoy the consistency that such rituals and traditions offer. So, to leverage this for everyone's benefit, try the following:

1. At the beginning of a new year, hand out holy cards of different saints to learners as they arrive.

2. Label individual seats with the corresponding saint's name from the holy cards.

3. Tell students to locate the seat that has their saint name posted on it.

This small, inexpensive gesture will help commemorate the first day of everyone gathering together and will more likely create immediate opportunities for new friendships to bloom.

Handing out holy cards to students can also elevate an occasion as one to be celebrated and remembered as extra special, similar to the tangible signs we receive to commemorate our experience on Palm Sunday and Ash Wednesday. The holy card ritual also connects the learners by the mere act of having a similar experience with one another. And, just as badges or tokens are given to learners in secular organizations as signs of their membership, saint holy cards can also be given to symbolize belonging to this group of learners. Everything we can do to promote such feelings will support our goal to build community, yet another vital hallmark of our faith life.

Saint Ignatius of Loyola

To further develop this experience, invite learners to keep their holy card in a safe place at home all year long. Their saint holy card is a small but personal sign of being a Catholic Christian. The following can help learners develop a closer relationship with their saint:

- Encourage students to ask that saint to pray for them, their families, and their community of learners. Be sure to choose a holy card for yourself and do the same.

- Share with your learners who your saint is, and let the learners know that you will be praying for each of them by name.

- Students with disabilities or those who have family members with disabilities may be interested to know that there are many saints who had disabilities or who are patron saints of certain disabilities. For example, St. Ignatius of Loyola suffered a disability in his leg, the convalescence of which drew him to God. St. Margaret of Castello was born with multiple disabilities, and St. Lucy was blinded. A detailed index of saints with disabilities is included on page 171 at the end of this book.

- Last, to encourage personal responsibility from the start, tell students that you want them to bring their saint holy card back on the last session of the year when everyone will receive a medal to keep. At that time, invite large-group sharing about how and where they kept their holy cards during the year. For those who didn't keep their holy card, allow them an opportunity to state why they had difficulty doing so (e.g., lost during a family move, blew away on the way home). Express your sincere gratitude to everyone for participating and for sharing their God-given gifts throughout the year. Acknowledge that each learner contributed positively to the greater good of the entire group.

REMEMBERING NAMES

As you begin your year, it can be difficult to learn and remember everyone's names. So, here's an idea to help you retain names as quickly as possible.

- Invite learners to fold a piece of paper in half lengthwise. Then, use a bold-point marker to create a personalized name tent.

- The name tent can be placed on a table, desk, or floor space in front of the student, facing you.

- Beyond sharing their names, invite learners also to share something about themselves (e.g., how many siblings they have, places they've lived, any pets they may have, etc.).

Be equally intentional about making time to introduce yourself. Share more than just your name. It may be especially interesting for others to hear why you decided to become a catechist or teacher. This will help your learners get to know you while simultaneously reminding yourself what inspired your passion and sustains your ministry today.

OPEN WITH SCRIPTURE OR LITERATURE

Another easy activity to initiate is to begin each session with a Scripture verse. You can use the verse in the following ways:

- Teach it as a song.

- Randomly ask for a volunteer to read or repeat it aloud.

- Ask students to say the verse as they exit for the day.

- Allow time for learners to discuss what the verse means to them. This can be done verbally, in writing, or through artwork. Providing alternative forms of expression allows the variety of gifts present to be uncovered and appreciated.

You may need to use the same verse repeatedly until it's memorized before incorporating a different verse.

You can also similarly incorporate literature about diversity into your teaching in ways that everyone can understand. There are many great children's books and fables that do this well. *The Rainbow Fish*, a favorite children's book, for example, conveys a story filled with lessons of love, sharing, and friendship. Stories such as this one help illustrate desired behaviors at all ages, and they contain moral truths that assist us in teaching social skills. They also raise awareness about and encourage appreciation of diverse learners.

> ## Scripture
>
> **Four Scripture verses to begin class and engage students:**
>
> - **Psalm 139:13–14**
> - **Leviticus 19:14**
> - **Galatians 4:13–14**
> - **John 14:34–35**

ENVIRONMENTAL CONSIDERATIONS

Everything in an environment sends a message, either directly or indirectly, about whether the space is warm and welcoming. Wall colors, lighting, sights, and sounds can all influence the affective feelings a learner or a parent may experience in your space. So, from the start of the year to the end, be mindful of ways you make every learner or guest feel welcome. For example, did you know that blue and green can help learners feel calm and that red and orange can make learners feel nervous and unsettled? The following are two tips to maintain a welcoming environment with posted materials:

- Post the schedule or agenda in the room and hand it out upon arrival. Doing so will provide added comfort, structure, and direction for some learners.

- If there are signs posted giving directions in the space, make sure they are written in a positive tone. State what learners are allowed to do, not what they are prohibited from doing.

Here are a few more ways to positively influence the affective experience of your learners.

- Choose a puzzle or book for students to enjoy when they've finished an assignment.

- Allow students to request or self-select a soother or fidget to aid attention (more on this topic in chapter 4).

- Stand by the desk or chair instead of sitting when you give instructions or work.

- Include a beanbag chair or some less structured furniture in the space and allow students to move to them.

- Create enough space around furniture so that a learner who uses a wheelchair can easily navigate it.

- Consider circular seating arrangements or small groupings of seating. Though seats in a row look neat and orderly, they may not make for easy access for all.

SUPPORT FROM THE CHURCH

A version of a saying you've probably heard is "Give a *learner* a fish, feed him for a day. Teach a learner to fish, feed him for life!" But before we can feed them, we must ensure that all learners can make it to the shore! If not, they will starve emotionally and spiritually from being alienated and excluded. In the United States Conference of Catholic Bishops' document *Welcome and Justice for Persons with Disabilities,* the bishops state, "Parish liturgical celebrations and catechetical programs should be accessible to persons with disabilities and open to their full, active and conscious participation, according to their capacity. Since the parish is the door to participation in the Christian experience, it is the responsibility of both pastors and laity to assure that those doors are always open. Costs must never be the controlling consideration limiting the welcome offered to those among us with disabilities, since provision of access to religious functions is a pastoral duty" (No. 5–6).

> Charleen, I just love your advocacy for giving learners the permission to leave their seats. So many power struggles have taken place over the years as instructors have insisted that students "sit still and stay in their seats" when it would have been better for everyone's attention and learning to allow them to *move!*

> Movement is good for the brain! We want thinkers, not sleepers! 😊 There's always a lot we can do to facilitate thinking beyond teaching the lesson. Most important, for catechesis to be effective (move the mind), it must first be affective (move the heart)!

Our mission and our ministry call us to work tirelessly to create full access to life in the Church for all. A person with a disability often has a very different trajectory in life than his or her peers have. Friends from their childhood will typically go on to get summer jobs, attend college, work professionally, get married, and start families. Unlike their peers, persons with disabilities will find their choices diminishing—especially if we do not create opportunities for building lifelong friendships and if we don't advocate for persons with disabilities to have a home in their faith community across their lives. Every learner is reason enough to offer a warm and welcoming place where he or she can feel safe and supported, but let us always remember that we may be entertaining saints or angels or God!

FURTHER RESOURCES AND LEARNING

To learn more about how you can best accommodate students with disabilities, visit

- *Archdiocese of Galveston-Houston's Ministry with Persons with Disabilities page, https://tinyurl.com/y8xeboew*

- *Archdiocese of Philadelphia's Religious Signs for Families app, www.deafcatholicphilly.org/religious-sign-app/*

- *Loyola Press's resources and curriculum for teaching and parenting children with disabilities, https://www.loyolapress.com/general/special-needs*

- *National Catholic Education Association's website, (NCEA), https://www.ncea.org/NCEA/. See also, NCEA's Exceptional Learner Resources page, https://tinyurl.com/yyxbm2lo*

- *National Catholic Office for the Deaf, www.ncod.org/resources*

- *National Catholic Partnership on Disability's website, www.ncpd.org.*

- *National Institute on Deafness and Other Communication Disorders, for information on how to sign "hello" in American Sign Language, https://www.nidcd.nih.gov/health/american-sign-language*

Three Takeaways

- We must work to cultivate a "ministry of presence" that says "I see you. I am present with you at this time and place, because God has ordained this meeting."

- We must take note of practical and simple ways we can cultivate an inviting and welcoming attitude and environment.

- We are called to work tirelessly to create inclusion opportunities and access to the Church for everyone.

 LOOKING AHEAD...

- After reading this chapter, what are a few ways you can respond in a welcoming way to the people God puts in front of you?

- What is your teaching style, and how might you adjust it after reading this chapter?

NOTES:

_____

_____

_____

_____

_____

_____

_____

CHAPTER 3
Recommended Learning Accommodations

BY JOHN E. BARONE

Getting Started

Imagine if this well-known Gospel story had gone a different way:

Great crowds had been following the Master for some time, and on one occasion, parents brought their children to him to be blessed. As they pressed around him, the mothers and fathers were filled with joy and hope, believing that the Master's touch could transform their children's lives.

The Apostles, seeing the great crush of people surrounding Jesus, began to criticize the parents, but Jesus stopped them: "No! Suffer the children to come unto me; don't stop them. Don't you know that the reign of God belongs to such as these?"

And so, the children gathered round him. And he blessed them and prayed over them. The parents were overjoyed, and the children beamed when he looked at them.

Except for Sarah. When it was her turn to see Jesus, she didn't return his loving gaze. She kept looking at the fidget spinner in her hand. "What do you have there, Sarah?" Jesus asked gently. "*Mine!*" she said, pulling her hand away.

"Sarah," the Master said compassionately, "if you want me to bless you, you're going to have to look me in the eye and put down that fidget spinner."

"*No!*" Sarah refused.

TWO-MINUTE CHECK-IN

- **How many students with disabilities does your classroom or church have in its programs?**

- **Have you seen students with disabilities and their families turned away or discouraged from finding help?**

- **Do you feel your school or parish is equipped to meet the needs of families of children with disabilities?**

Jesus shook his head in disappointment and called for the parents. "I'm sorry, but I can't bless her if she won't even look at me. She refuses to follow my instructions. And she's obviously not gaining anything by being here with me. All she cares about is that fidget spinner. Please take her home." The parents sighed and made their way through the crowd with their little girl.

The next child, Joshua, smiled at Jesus, looked him in the eye, and wrapped his arms around Jesus' neck. Jesus was very pleased and began to bless him. But suddenly, Joshua started making hooting noises. Jesus said, "Please stop that, Joshua." The other children laughed, and Joshua stopped hooting for a little while.

Then Joshua's head began to twitch. And he hooted again. Jesus said to his parents, "I'm sorry, but Joshua's noises and twitches are disrupting the blessings. He can control it, because he stopped when I asked him to. He's making the other children uncomfortable. I don't think he can stay." Joshua and his family looked humiliated as they walked away.

Martha was next, but Benjamin was so excited to see Jesus that he pushed past her and knocked her down. Martha began to scream uncontrollably. She yelled, "IT'S NOT FAIR! I was next! It's not his turn!" Jesus signaled to both sets of parents, who picked up their children and walked away. Martha's screams could still be heard as Jesus smiled and welcomed the next appropriately behaving child.

The Gospel of the Lord?

Does this sound like the Jesus you know? When Jesus said, "The reign of God belongs to such as these," do you suppose there was an unwritten qualifier that read "Except for those with ADHD, social-development problems, self-regulation issues, physical and verbal tics, mood disorders, and any other disability that would impact their functioning"?

Definitely not. Jesus made every effort to reach out to those who were different, marginalized, and troubled. He would not have turned these young people away. So, why do youth with disabilities so frequently find it difficult to be included in our schools, faith formation, and youth-ministry programs? And why do some of us find it difficult to welcome them?

Your reimagining of this Gospel story is excellent on many levels! Jesus, the Master Catechist, is the model for us all. We are called to offer the same unconditional love to every person our Father puts in front of us, with no qualifiers!! ALL are welcome, and we need to remember that the God who invited them is the same God who invited us!

Absolutely. There's no way Jesus would turn those kids away. He'd probably be delighted with their quirks!

I know he always has been with mine and yours! 😊

Differentiating Learning and Providing Accommodations

Financial struggles, lack of training, and fear of those who are different are just a few of the many reasons some of our faith communities may close their doors to individuals with disabilities. Also high on that list are rigid styles of old-school pedagogy, which insist that learners accommodate to the system and not vice versa. Individuals with disabilities are often unable to be successful in programs that do not accommodate their needs or modify the curriculum to be more accessible. And when they fail, some are removed with inadequate approximations of inclusion, such as giving the parent copies of the textbook to provide formation at home or warehousing the student to a separate space with little community interaction.

When young people are struggling with these differences, the last thing they need is to be rejected by their church or school. But they are not the only ones hurt by this—exclusion deprives everyone of the challenge and benefit of learning to accept others regardless of their differences and learning from other perspectives. We are all made better by being together.

As educators, we must follow in the footsteps of Jesus, welcoming all of God's children by providing accommodations and modifications where needed. Our responsibility as teachers, catechists, or parents is to present the Good News in a variety of styles and levels of complexity and to be open to modifying the curriculum to match the different levels of our learners' functioning.

NEW METHODOLOGIES

Traditional methodology assumes that students will accommodate to the teaching institution—and not the other way around. All students have to follow the same procedures, use the same methods, and adhere to the same guidelines. Educators are now recognizing the value of offering accommodations and modifications to students, as these implementations lead to improved achievement, inclusion, and retention. In the faith-formation sphere, these accommodations and modifications help us welcome all of God's children—including those with disabilities—for if there is any place where all should be welcome, it is church!

ACCOMMODATIONS VERSUS MODIFICATIONS

When a student receives a diagnosis of a disability, accommodations and modifications are often recommended to help the student succeed in areas that are impacted by the disability. Their evaluation reports can be a bit confusing, as sometimes the terms *accommodation* and *modification* are used interchangeably.

An accommodation allows a student to do the same work that the other students are doing but in a different way. A modification is a change in the assignment itself in response to a student's developmental abilities. For example, many students are required to name the fruits of the Holy Spirit in preparation for Confirmation. An accommodation might allow a student to use pictograms to identify the fruits. The student is still completing the requirements, just with a little extra support. A modification might entail asking the student to name a few of the fruits of the Holy Spirit.

In another example, if a teacher assigned twenty pages of reading and four questions to answer, an accommodation wouldn't change the assignment, but it would change how the work is done. The learner would still be responsible for completing the work, though more time would be given to complete the assignment. Other accommodations could include asking someone to read to the student or record his or her answers.

A great example of a catechetical program that meets the needs of all students and includes modified lessons is the *Adaptive Finding God Program* by Loyola Press. *Adaptive Finding God* offers faith formation for diverse learners that can be customized for different learning settings. The program provides teachers, catechists, and parents with multisensory tools, support, and guidance to effectively respond to the strengths and abilities of each student. The interactive curriculum can be used alongside the *Finding God* grade-level books or as a stand-alone program for parishes, schools, and homes.

Love it! What a great resource!

Modifications might include reducing the number of pages to read or questions to answer. Students with disabilities may be asked to do less or a different assignment altogether, depending on their ability. Modifications are appropriate when the original assignment is beyond the abilities of the student. They could include

- fewer questions or tasks than the standard assignment.
- shorter length of the task or assignment.
- alternative task within the developmental ability of the student.

PARENTAL CONSIDERATIONS

Sometimes parents are open about sharing the recommended accommodations and modifications for their child with disabilities and sometimes not. You may not see these recommendations due to confidentiality reasons. In other cases, parents won't disclose information because they don't want their loved one to be labeled or because they find it difficult to accept that their child has a disability. Whatever the case, we must be open to allowing all learners to participate to the extent that they are able and include everyone in God's house. Our flexibility in providing accommodations and modifications for students opens the door to those who otherwise could not keep up with the demands of the program. Accommodations and modifications can also be offered to students who demonstrate the need but haven't yet received a diagnosis. In the next section, we'll provide strategies on how to accommodate students regardless of whether you've received an official evaluation report.

Modifications for Students with Disabilities

Since celebrating sacraments is a priority for Catholics, consider these modifications for students with disabilities who are preparing to celebrate:

- Practice with unconsecrated hosts in preparation for First Communion.
- Teach "prayer hands" for the "Amen" response.
- Have an adult accompany individuals with disabilities in the Reconciliation room, though under the same "seal."
- Allow candidates to copy a sample letter to the pastor requesting to be confirmed.
- Provide alternatives to communal celebrations if they would cause undue anxiety.
- Offer retreats for families of children with disabilities on a single day.

RECOMMENDED ACCOMMODATIONS

Extended Time

Disabilities can significantly increase the amount of time needed to complete a task, particularly if a student has high levels of distractibility and/or anxiety. Some students also need more time to think. Teachers and catechists can accommodate these needs by increasing the wait time after asking a question. Instead of calling on students who have a faster processing speed—and whose hands typically fly up after a question is asked—give plenty of "thinking time" to allow those who process slowly to come up with the answer. Another helpful technique is to preview the question for the student, giving him or her time to think about it while talking with another student and then returning to solicit the answer.

Educators could also support students with this accommodation by increasing the time they have to complete a short- or long-term project, allowing them to work at their own pace. Many students find it helpful to divide large projects into smaller chunks, working on more manageable steps rather than trying to tackle the big project all at once. Catechists and teachers can ask parents of a child with a disability how much extra time their child may need to complete a project. Allowing multiple completion options for students instead of one class deadline will help alleviate the stigma a student may feel in completing an assignment after everyone else.

Creating a "Break Area"

Allowing students the freedom to take scheduled or as-needed breaks in their work can make a huge difference in their ability to participate fully. Creating a comfortable "break area" in the learning space provides the opportunity to temporarily disconnect from the larger group, spend some time away, and come back refreshed and ready to participate.

Creating your break area may take some coordination with others who share the learning space. The space should be designed to feel safe and "apart" but still within sight of the adult supervising. You may consider placing a small couch, beanbag chair, or soft cushions in a corner of the space. Since it also serves as a "calm down" area, be sure not to have any sharp items such as scissors or pencils there.

Break Area Benefits for Individuals with ADHD and Autism

- The break area can be used by students with ADHD who have reached the limit of their ability to pay attention and need time to refocus.

- Students with autism benefit from the opportunity to take emotional regulation breaks to calm themselves and prevent meltdowns.

- Those with anxiety disorders can rely on the break area to soothe themselves and manage anxious thoughts.

- This special space can also be a refuge for anyone who is finding it difficult to function and needs a little time away to self-regulate.

A TEACHER'S GUIDE TO STUDENT BREAK AREAS

If it's not possible to have a break area in your learning space, you can still allow students to take kinesthetic breaks, inviting them to go to the back of the room to stretch, move around, regain focus, and self-regulate.

Here are a few ways to encourage students to take a break:

1. **Teaching and Practice:** Before learners begin to use the break area, be sure to teach them how to use it. Share guidelines for taking a break, and practice these steps.

2. **Initiation:** If students are able to recognize their own signs of needing a break (losing focus, feeling hyperactive, having emotional dysregulation), they can initiate their own breaks, either by asking for permission or by walking to the break area. This is ideal, as you want learners to take ownership of their needs, but sometimes learners are unable to recognize these signs or to initiate the break. If this is the case, you can prompt the learner by asking, "Would you like to take a break?" or arrange a break signal or "break card" (an object that signifies permission to take a break). Be sure to practice beginning and ending a break quietly and in a way that doesn't distract other learners. Never use the break as a punishment for misbehavior—the area should be viewed as a positive, calming space.

3. **Supervision:** Because students who need breaks are often in a state of upset, it's important that you vigilantly supervise the break area to ensure that the student is safe and is using the space effectively.

4. **Break Tools:** Having a variety of tools on hand to help a learner refocus and calm down provides practice in self-soothing. You could include a white board with dry-erase markers for drawing or writing, a white-noise machine, stress balls and other sensory tools, audio players, noise-reduction headphones, binders with calming pictures, or pictograms for different calming and refocusing strategies.

5. **Sensory Supplies:** Students with sensory-integration differences often benefit from having access to a "soother station," which includes stress balls, putty, and other fidget items. I strongly recommend that you prohibit fidget spinners or cubes, unless they are used during breaks when there is no need to focus on something else, as they typically distract students even more. Other sensory supplies that are helpful are stretchy bands to loop around a desk or chair legs that students can push against, and weighted blankets, lap belts, or vests. For more suggested sensory supplies, please see chapter 4. You can store sensory items in the break area and main learner area.

6. **Response Alternatives:** When taking a survey or quiz, do you prefer to answer orally or in writing? Offering students these same options allows them to respond to assignments in their preferred style. For children with disabilities, response options could also include dictating their answers to someone else to write down or record or using a laptop, phone, or tablet to record answers.

7. **Preferential Seating:** You probably know what the conventional wisdom says about where to move a student who is struggling to pay attention. Yes, that's right, the front row! While that can be helpful for some, the front row can be the worst place for students with disabilities. Some learning spaces have a bank of windows behind the teaching area with an outdoor view, which can be distracting—and probably not the best place for a student with attention differences. Students with high anxiety may feel "exposed" or "too close" to the teacher or catechist. Others hyperfocus on the teacher and don't reference others in the room. Consider how you feel when you're sitting in the front row in a movie theater. For some students, a desk in the front row feels just as uncomfortable.

Finding optimal placement for a person with disabilities also applies to church. The front pews are sometimes the best area for attention, but if the learner has a disability that may be distracting, like a physical and/or verbal tic, another area might be better. Students who are hyperactive and need frequent kinesthetic breaks would be best seated at the end of the pew for easy exits and returns.

Who do you think would know best where a young person should sit? Many times, it's the individual learner. Students can be coached in surveying the learning space to determine the optimal place to be, individualized to meet their needs.

A STUDENT'S GUIDE TO PREFERENTIAL SEATING

When coaching students to choose their seat, you can use this guide to help them decide the best place. Invite learners to consider the following factors:

- **Décor:** Are there bright, distracting, sparkly things within sight? Could you move to where you wouldn't see those objects or pictures?

- **Air Conditioning and Heating Vents:** Does the noise of the AC vents distract you or make it difficult to hear? Are they bothering you by blowing in your face? Let's find a less windy spot.

- **The Door:** How close is your seat to the entrance and exit of the room? Do you find it distracting when students open and close the door? Do the noises outside the room distract you? Maybe it would be best to get away from that door!

- **The Windows:** How's the view? Is it distracting? Do you find yourself always looking outside instead of focusing on the lesson? Can you sit with your back to the window?

- **Other Students:** Are other students distracting? Disruptive? Are they having private conversations that make it difficult for you to focus? Or are you having private conversations with them? Whom could you sit with to help you focus better?

- **The Catechist or Teacher:** Where does the catechist or teacher usually stand? Do you learn better closer to him or her or farther away? How does the distance from this person affect your focus? Find that "just right" distance for your seat.

- **Your Sensory Abilities:** Do you have a disability with sight or hearing? Would you see or hear better if you moved closer to the front? If you have a cochlear implant, would it be helpful to sit on the side of the room that corresponds to the side where your implant is located?

- **Your Feelings:** Are there areas of the room where you feel more or less anxious? Choose the seat that makes you feel the most calm, safe, and confident.

REMEMBER, IT'S FOR THE KIDS

One final reason more isn't being done to accommodate youth with disabilities is that it's hard work. Differentiating the curriculum and providing accommodations can be challenging and take time and effort. Many schools and faith-formation programs find it easier to have one system, one set of expectations and procedures, and require everyone to follow them. But the cost is the loss of those precious children in our community—just like the ones in the opening story who were sent away. Be horrified by the exclusion. Do the work it takes to make inclusion happen.

Welcome all learners, as much as possible. Get to know them and their families. Determine their strengths and their challenges. Become comfortable with their quirks and differences. Seek out training opportunities to improve your teaching. Use inclusive catechetical programs like *Adaptive Finding God*. Don't insist that all learners do everything the same way. Provide them with the tools, the permission, and the practice to understand the way they learn best and to grow in ownership of their learning and development. Let all the children come.

Providing accommodations to learners with disabilities is a very individualized ministry. We can't say that enough. Each person requires his or her own tools and practices. Simply put, not everyone needs glasses, and if they do, they certainly don't need the same glasses! A group of 25 learners may include three to five students who require modifications and/or accommodations, but only one or two may require the exact same one.

Absolutely. Some catechists and teachers may find it intimidating to keep track of who needs what, but it's essential that they do, because these disabilities interfere with a person's ability to learn.

That's why we pray this book is a lifeline for those who want to be better prepared to serve all kiddos!

Three Takeaways

- **Welcoming all learners with disabilities, as well as their loved ones, is an important part of our calling as Catholics and of our ministry as educators.**

- **Get to know each learner individually to determine the accommodations and modifications that will best fit him or her.**

- **Determine which tools you can have on hand to create opportunities for self-soothing and break time.**

 ## LOOKING AHEAD...

◆ How will you change your learning environment to accommodate individuals with disabilities?

◆ What accommodations and modifications would be helpful to provide?

◆ How can you be more like Jesus in welcoming all types of learners?

✳ **NOTES:**

_____

_____

_____

_____

_____

_____

_____

CHAPTER 4
Integrating Sensory Supports into Your Teaching

BY CHARLEEN KATRA

Getting Started

What would you do if your pastor told you that some parishioners who have children with disabilities were choosing to attend another church several miles away because of its disability-ministry program? You would probably want to investigate why this church's program was drawing families from other denominations.

TWO-MINUTE CHECK-IN

- What does your parish or classroom setting look like?

- Do you feel that it accommodates diverse learners?

- When you were a student, what best helped you learn? What environment best suited your needs?

Actually, it's not uncommon for families who have a loved one with a disability to travel great distances to participate in programs and events that are offered specifically for them. This reality is often indicative of how few programs and events are intentionally created with full access and inclusion in mind. If we want to eliminate a family's need to seek spiritual support elsewhere, we must look seriously and carefully at what we are or are not offering them at our parishes, from faith formation and liturgies to schools and community-building events.

FEATURES OF A MODEL DISABILITY PROGRAM

I had the chance to tour a church that was drawing families to its disability-ministry program, which proved helpful in generating ideas. From the friendly welcome given to every person who walked through their doors to the spirit of generosity that they communicated in sharing information about their program, I could already sense the attraction—and that was just upon arriving at their property. The following best practices and strategies crystallize why so many families were drawn to the church:

Active Disability-Ministry Committee and Funding

This church had formed a committee to design programs and physical spaces that would be most conducive to including individuals who learn and behave in diverse ways. The implementation of their program was well-organized and incorporated strategies and best practices commonly used in other churches and educational settings. They also established a dependable buddy system and frequent rotation between different activities or centers (Vacation Bible School format), etc. By the end of the tour, it became evident that this church had large amounts of funds and space at its disposal.

Sensory Rooms and Intentionally Designed Spaces

In most churches, money and space are both limited and, hence, highly coveted. Space is often shared between ministries, and funding for desired resources is usually challenging to obtain. Even so, with all I observed on the tour, the intentionally designed rooms were the standout—and most necessary—component. One room included a floor-to-ceiling Lava lamp that vibrated when hugged. On one wall, a video projected a relaxing beach scene with waves gently crashing on the sand. Comfortable furniture (e.g., beanbag chairs and couches), soft lighting, swings, tunnels, padded mats, and mirrors filled the space. These rooms are commonly referred to as "sensory rooms" because they contain a variety of large- and small-scale sensory-integration manipulatives. Sensory rooms offer a positive, relaxing, or therapeutic space for individuals with sensory-processing disorders— but they can be enjoyed by others, too! A group of occupational therapists, pediatricians, and special educators had planned the ideal space for this specialized ministry.

THE BENEFITS OF INCLUSION EFFORTS

You might wonder if such intentional effort and expense are really beneficial. In short, yes. Intentional efforts not only benefit the learner but also help achieve the end goal of welcoming and supporting the whole family so they can regularly attend church together. Individuals who learn differently can have varied educational, behavioral, and emotional needs, some similar to one another, some unique. One important area of concern within the disability community is sensory integration. When the sensory-integration process is working effectively, it enables human beings to respond appropriately to their environment.

UNDERSTANDING OUR SENSORY SYSTEMS

There are seven identified sensory systems that appear on the chart provided on the next page. The bodily location and function of each system are also indicated there. Though these sensory systems affect every one of us, no two of us have the same sensory needs. Therefore, our ability to understand effective sensory-based interventions for individuals who struggle with an unbalanced sensory system is imperative if we are to successfully advocate for their full inclusion in parish, educational, liturgical, and social settings.

Our brain's job is to process all the varied input such as sights, sounds, and smells that we are experiencing at every moment. This act of processing sensory input is accomplished easily for many of us, sometimes effortlessly. You may be reading this text seemingly undistracted right now. But it's almost certain that there are several sensory experiences happening around you at the same time. You may need to pay serious attention, especially if you are one of the one-in-six people who struggle with sensory-processing issues.

SENSORY EXPERIENCE

Stop reading for a moment and focus on your immediate environment. What do you notice? Do you hear a conversation nearby, the hum of a refrigerator, the sounds of street traffic? Do you feel a cool breeze from a fan or the warmth from a heater on your skin? Is the lighting bright or is this page too white? Do you smell food being prepared or a fragranced candle burning? Has a door closed or a faucet dripped? How many sensations is your brain experiencing at the same time?

When we intentionally stop and observe the flood of sensory input—much of which may be occurring simultaneously—we will likely become impressed by and grateful for our brain's ability to organize and respond efficiently to all these stimuli. Hopefully, our increased awareness will help us recognize just how challenging everyday life experiences are for individuals whose ability to process sensory input is a liability and not an asset. Imagine not being able to disregard or separate a multitude of sensory inputs, or having each sensation magnified with little to no relief. We can begin to appreciate how the stress and anxiety levels of individuals living with sensory-processing disorders are exacerbated by such a constant onslaught of sensations. We can also realize how extremely challenging home, church, school, and community settings can be for them.

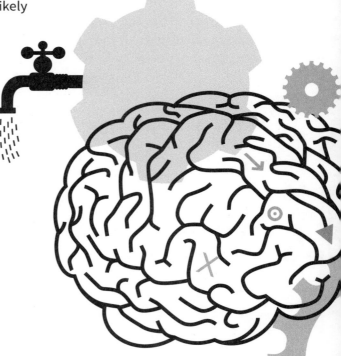

Sensory Experience Chart

System	Location	Function	Application for a person with autism, et al.
Tactile *(touch)*	Skin	Provides information about the environment and object qualities (touch, pressure, texture, hard, soft, sharp, dull, heat, cold, pain).	Touch can be painful: don't touch without asking, and don't "surprise" touch. May prefer not to share a sign of peace, receive ashes, sign oneself with holy water, or be blessed with chrism oil. Practice needed.
Vestibular *(balance)*	Inner ear	Provides information about where our body is in space and whether or not we or our surroundings are moving. Tells about speed and direction of movement.	Crowded hallways, gyms, churches, etc., can be challenging: allow early or late arrival or dismissal to avoid a learner being bumped and becoming upset.
Proprioception *(body awareness)*	Muscles and joints	Provides information about where a certain body part is and how it is moving.	Relates to postures in Mass: standing, kneeling, bowing, genuflecting; going to communion; sharing a sign of peace and signing oneself. Also, using playground equipment.
Visual *(sight)*	Retina of the eye	Provides information about objects and persons. Helps us define boundaries as we move through time and space.	Pay attention to bright lighting: may cause stimming (hand flapping) or blinking, which can be visual signs/cues that someone is trying to gain focus or de-stress.
Auditory *(hearing)*	Inner ear	Provides information about sounds in the environment (loud, soft, high, low, near, far).	When sounds hurt, people shut down or become angry. Higher frequencies are more irritating; some people prefer deeper voices. Also consider fire alarms, loud music, large, noisy gatherings.
Gustatory *(taste)*	Tongue	Provides information about different types of taste (sweet, sour, bitter, salty, spicy).	Relates to receiving the Body and Blood of Christ in the Eucharist, consuming beverages, snacks, and meals.
Olfactory *(smell)*	Nose	Provides information about different types of smell (musty, acrid, putrid, flowery, pungent).	Relates to the use of incense, the presence of floral arrangements, the smell of perfumes and colognes, markers, and aromas of snack foods and cafeteria meals.

Adapted from Brenda Smith Myles, *Asperger Syndrome and Sensory Issues: Practical Solutions for Making Sense of the World,* (Shawnee Mission, MS: Autism Asperger Publishing Company, 2000), 5. Reprinted with permission.

Implementing Sensory Solutions in Your Parish

Is your faith community among the majority of churches who desire to start or enhance their disability-ministry efforts, despite limited space and funds? Would your parish, school, or home benefit from having a collection of sensory items available to aid successful learning? If so, you may want to consider the solution described below. If a dedicated sensory room is not an option, consider investing in a Traveling Sensory Kit, a tool kit that offers a variety of sensory stimulation to meet the needs of individuals wherever they are: church, classroom, retreat center, living room, playground, soccer field, etc. Below is a list of items successfully used in some Catholic parishes. These items can directly support and promote the full inclusion of parishioners or visitors.

TRAVELING SENSORY KIT

This entire collection can fit comfortably inside a rolling suitcase or duffel bag, which offers flexibility in storing the manipulatives as well as transporting them to be shared across parish ministries. At an estimated total cost of five hundred dollars, these resources will help minimize the requirements for additional space and funds to better serve all learners. You may choose to purchase them all at once, or each item could be obtained individually, based on the needs presented. Above each section, you will see the presented need. A learner may verbalize the need or could simply present a card to request a particular item without speaking. Printed cards containing this information can be included in the pockets of the suitcase or duffel bag to make contents as user-friendly as possible.

Presented need: difficulty sitting or staying seated

 **Sensory solution: inflatable stability wobble cushion.** These inflatable disks can be used as chair cushions for individuals who are hyperactive and need to calm down and focus. The ability to adjust the inflation level and the choice between a smooth or knobby sitting surface make this item flexible to the needs (proprioceptive or tactile) of each individual.

 **Sensory solution: elastic bands.** Use elastic bands on the front legs of a desk or chair to provide a way for the student to move his or her legs while remaining seated. This ability to move will help students stay on task for longer periods of time while also providing an active release for their stress or anxiety.

The Adaptive Teacher ➜ Faith-Based Strategies to Reach and Teach Learners with Disabilities

Sensory solution: weighted lap pad or blanket. Weighted pads and blankets fill the need for sensory input that helps users develop body awareness. These pads, when placed on learners' laps, help improve attention and concentration and have a calming effect on the individual, which may also reduce meltdowns. A lap pad can help an individual stay seated for longer time spans and can be used almost anywhere. The weight of the pad should not exceed 10 percent of the user's weight.

Sensory solution: folding trampoline. Sometimes, releasing some energy jumping on a trampoline will have a calming effect on an individual. This activity also helps circulate oxygenated blood, boost the metabolism, and develop motor skills and coordination. Individuals can simply stand and balance on the bouncy surface, walk in place, or bounce and jump on the trampoline. Ensure the safety of the user by providing a well-lit space for its use, having enough space around the unit, and having learners take turns "spotting" each other while using it.

Presented need: fidgeting or difficulty concentrating

Sensory solution: plastic coil fidget. This tool can be used when learners need something to occupy their hands for better focus and comprehension. It is quiet and small enough to be used by a learner without distracting others.

Sensory solution: puffer balls. Squishy strands of rubber bound to form a ball that is easy to grasp and stimulating to hold. The interesting texture and ever-changing form of this ball are great for relieving stress and can be used for hand therapy.

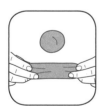

Sensory solution: stretchy ball. This ball forms to whatever shape the user gives it by squeezing, stretching, or simply holding it. It can be used with learners who will benefit from having a soothing texture or fidgety object in their hand. It can serve to relieve stress as well.

Sensory solution: chewable pencil toppers. For individuals with oral sensory needs, chewable pencil toppers are a safe modification. Pencil toppers fit on standard pencils. Individuals with this need will benefit from the calming, self-regulating effects of having something to chew on. Having this chewable implement available can improve their focus as well. It would be a good idea to have several, as these become personal items once used by an individual.

 **Sensory solution: sensory fidget mat.** Sensory fidget mats are used by placing them on a flat surface within reach of the hands or feet of the user, who can touch and fidget using the mat while performing a task. The stimulating bumps and surface texture help calm individuals who use them. They may aid in improving concentration as well.

Presented need: to soothe anxiety or hyperactivity

 **Sensory solution: fiber-optic fountain lamp.** These lights can help an individual relax by providing visual and tactile stimulation. Use in a low-light environment and invite the individual to gently touch the fiber-optic strands to give motion to the lamp light. Some fiber-optic fountain lamps have "rotate" and "pulse" settings. Try different settings until a favorable effect is reached.

 **Sensory solution: liquid bubble timer.** The combination of vibrant color and the liquid motion of this timer can help individuals relax by focusing on the drops as they move to the bottom of the timer. Also useful for limiting the time dedicated to an activity or helping individuals develop a concept of time with a visual representation.

 **Sensory solution: wax motion lamp.** These lamps have a slow, soothing motion that stimulates individuals with calming visual input. To aid the effectiveness of these tools, dim the lighting in the room and add soft music or calming sounds. Watching the motion of the melted wax also helps individuals develop eye-tracking abilities.

 **Sensory solution: plush figure.** One of the *Adaptive Finding God* Learning Tools from Loyola Press, the plush Jesus the Teacher figure is a concrete way for learners to connect with our Lord and the Catholic faith. It is especially beneficial for children who are tactile-kinesthetic and visual learners, and it can be used in a variety of ways. For example, it can bring comfort, be held during prayer services, brought to Mass, or taken home to share in everyday activities (e.g., at family dinner or a sporting event). A plush Mary Our Mother figure is also available from Loyola Press.

Presented need: environment is too loud or bright

 **Sensory solution: lightweight folding stereo headphones.** These headphones can be used with or without audio input to lower the environmental noise. If using with audio, test the volume before offering them to the user. Allow the user to wear them however they feel most comfortable, including upside down (with the band under the chin), or with one or both ears uncovered by the pads.

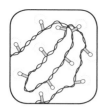 **Sensory solution: string lights.** String lights come in different varieties. Choose a set that has the option of color-changing LED bulbs and a variety of operation modes (e.g., waves, sequential, twinkle, steady, and slow-fade). Use by dimming overhead lighting and modulating with string lights according to the specific needs of the individual. Adjust the operation mode and colors for the desired effect: faster settings can stimulate and excite while slower or steady settings can have a calming effect.

Presented need: something exciting to focus on

 **Sensory solution: perpetual-motion machine.** A moving, battery-operated sculpture that stays in motion once started. Some designs have colorful balls that spin around a central axis; others have weighted rings on multiple axes which move independent of one another. Choose one that will be interesting to individuals seeking exciting stimuli.

 **Sensory solution: LED strobe bulb.** LED strobe bulbs are available from various manufacturers. They are easy to install in any standard light fixture; some are even compatible with dimmer switches. Use with individuals who seek exciting visual stimuli. **Caution:** *Do not use* with individuals who have seizures.

Presented need: learning timing or a sequence

 **Sensory solution: visual timer.** A visual timer gives a child a simple, tangible object to aid in developing an awareness of time as it elapses. Color coding on the timer can help an individual visualize the remaining time and how much has elapsed. This item can help an individual set and keep a time limit on an activity or break. It can also help calm individuals if they are anxious about how long they will need to stay somewhere or do an activity.

 **Sensory solution: flip book or picture cards.** *My Picture Missal* Flip Book and Mass Picture Cards are used during Mass to walk children through the parts of the liturgy, providing interactive cues for actions and gestures. *My Picture Missal* Flip Book and Mass Picture Cards are ideal for those with diverse learning styles, preschool and kindergarten classes, baptismal preparation programs, preschool mothers' groups, Liturgy of the Word for children, and parishioners with young children.

STORING SENSORY ITEMS

When sensory items are not being used, you will want to thoroughly clean them before storing them in a cool, dry place. For a traveling sensory kit, be sure to purchase a duffel bag or rolling suitcase large enough to hold all the items. The sensory items you acquire will be helpful only if they are accessible, so be sure to let others know where they're stored and how they can obtain them. If you have available space, you can create a room or dedicate a section of a room for storing the items. If not, you'll want to designate a specific area where the items can be retrieved during programs or events. Consider calling this space the "calming corner" or, even better, the "Christ corner," as the sensory items put flesh on the welcome and love of Christ extended to all persons. These titles can also be suggestions for the rooms in the back of church sanctuaries often referred to as "cry rooms." The sharing or expanding of the usage of this space would benefit many families, especially if a collection of fidgets is available there too.

SENSORY TOOLS, NOT TOYS

Remember to teach students that soothers and sensory items are tools, not toys. At first glance, many may believe otherwise. We want to support ownership and independence of our learners in understanding and addressing their own sensory needs. The more we educate and advocate for those with sensory issues, the more peaceful and cohesive our educational, liturgical, and home settings will be.

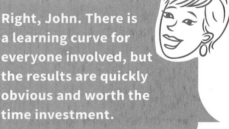

Charleen, I think it's important to note that learners with disabilities should gradually take ownership of the use of these items rather than have full freedom to use them immediately. Catechists will need to teach students how to access and use the items appropriate to their sensory needs and coach them as they learn to use the items effectively.

Right, John. There is a learning curve for everyone involved, but the results are quickly obvious and worth the time investment.

CREATING INDIVIDUALIZED SENSORY ACCOMMODATIONS

Here's a question for you: what do roller coasters and Brussels sprouts have in common? At first consideration, seemingly nothing. But in the context of sensory input, they have everything in common. It is important to remember that we are all constantly processing sensory input. Some individuals may have a greater ability to do so, but each person will still have some things they crave or resist. And roller coasters and Brussels sprouts are often categorized as things people either do or do not like, often with great intensity. Though each offers a combination of different sensory inputs, both provide some with enjoyment and others with loathing.

Sensory processing is an intensely individualized act that determines what is craved or resisted. Here's how to accommodate those personal preferences in a number of settings.

In Liturgy. In liturgical settings, the number of people, the music, the bells, or even the incense can affect someone adversely. To help, seat this person at the end of the pew, which will allow easy access to walkways if a break is needed.

In the Classroom. In instructional settings, including retreats and conferences, pay attention to overhead and stage lighting, room temperatures, available furniture, and the number of attendees. Can some of the lights be dimmed or eliminated? Is there alternative seating available that is less structured?

At Events. Consider providing a "calming area" at events where large crowds are present. You can also check with attendees regarding room temperatures. Sometimes the planners are working up a sweat and don't realize others feel cold, making it difficult to pay attention.

So glad you are including this, Charleen. It's common for sensory issues to look like behavioral issues, and when adults try to use firm discipline, it's like throwing gasoline on the fire!

Absolutely true, John! We want folks to think "fidget first," because a little fidget goes a long way to resolving big issues!

BEST PRACTICES FOR INTRODUCING SENSORY ITEMS

Incorporating a sensory item is always intended to be a solution to a real need—not create additional ones. Consider the following points before introducing sensory items to learners:

Introduce Sensory Items to Everyone

You will want to introduce the sensory items to the person they are intended for as well as to other individuals who may not need them. Taking the time to identify specific items and their target usage will help deter any difficulties or harm being caused to the intended user, such as the items being misused or becoming a distraction.

Make Sure Sensory Supports Are Available

Having items available and accessible provides individuals with the ability to select what they need when they need it. Adult self-advocates often report that they were aware, even as a young person, when they were on the verge of losing control emotionally or behaviorally. Unfortunately, their sensory needs often went unnoticed and unmet, leading to confusion, frustration, or something worse. So, knowing where helpful items are located and having permission to get one when needed provides a positive choice. This leads to a better reality while also affirming a person's independence and increasing self-esteem. Conversely, you may choose an item you know will benefit someone and bring it to that person, or choose one for yourself!

Talk to the Family

Once you learn or suspect that an individual has a sensory need, have a conversation with him or her, or the parent or guardian as appropriate. The information you receive will often help you select the item(s) that will be most beneficial. You will likely be informed that there are already specific items or activities being used by the family in the home or other settings. This is ideal information to know because we want to allow the learner to bring what is already working, if appropriate, or we want to replicate it if possible. Sensory seeking can affect people of all ages and all abilities.

Create a Strategy

Once a specific need is identified, strategies can be implemented to help stimulate or calm an individual, allowing the person to function successfully at school, at work, or at play. For example, adding a set of elastic bands to the front legs of a desk or chair offers a person the chance to move his or her legs while seated, which serves the desired ability to remain seated longer.

Note the Individual's Age

Be sensitive to the age-appropriateness of any item or strategy as it relates to respecting the chronological age of the individual as well as the developmental level. A teenager may receive better assistance from fidgeting with a Rubik's Cube or a Hacky Sack than from an item that looks like it was designed for a young child. You will want to monitor both the effectiveness of the fidget and how acceptable the item is socially for the individual. For example, during a video-recorded meeting, rubber bands were placed in front of every chair around a boardroom table to provide the perfect fidget for attendees while they listened and processed important information. Without the bands, they would have noisily clicked their pens as a go-to, unconscious behavior—not ideal for a recording. Noting this reality reminds us that even simply squeezing a stress ball can assist many people—young or old—to focus better while processing some of life's daily activities.

SELECTING THE RIGHT FIDGET

Sensory items called "fidgets" are smaller manipulatives that are often beneficial in helping a person remain calm or focus on the task at hand. To select an ideal fidget for the student, consider the following:

- Look for fidgets that provide the appropriate sensory input (calming or alerting).
- Identify fidgets that are safe, quiet, and portable so that they can be used in a variety of public environments.
- Knowledge of a learner's fine-motor skills and strength will help determine whether he or she would prefer holding the plush Jesus or a smaller, harder manipulative.
- The best items are the ones individuals express interest in. That will be the motivating factor to keep them peacefully tuned into their surroundings.

Add to your sensory kit collection on a continuing basis, because the more items there are to choose from, the more needs you will be able to meet.

USING SENSORY SUPPORTS IN FAITH FORMATION

We can also address the sensory issues that relate to formation needs within the Church.

First Holy Communion: When preparing individuals to receive the Eucharist, utilize the unconsecrated hosts—even the smallest piece, if that is all one can accept. Knowing what to expect regarding the taste and texture of the host will greatly assist in making the celebration of this sacrament the joyful experience it's meant to be.

Baptism: When teaching about Baptism, use a baby doll and a bowl of water to depict a Baptism. Provide a font with holy water for individuals to sign themselves as they enter or leave the space.

Confirmation: An invaluable step to include when preparing individuals for Confirmation is practicing the act of signing a cross on their forehead. This will prepare the candidates for the feel of the bishop's hand on their forehead as he performs this same action during the Rite of Confirmation using sacred chrism oil. This oil is very fragrant, and allowing those preparing to smell it in advance is advisable, though you will need to use baby oil instead during practice sessions. The wet, slippery texture of the baby oil will be a very helpful similar sensation for diverse learners to experience before the actual celebration. You may also want to direct the candidate to look to the side if the visual experience of someone's hand coming toward him or her is difficult to accept. Always advise clergy in advance of individual differences or assistance that may be needed during celebrations.

Sensory Supports from Our Faith

Our Catholic faith provides a variety of items that can also be incorporated into your sensory kit collection.

- If an individual is comfortable carrying around a strand of Mardi Gras beads, offer a rosary, which has beads too.

- If allergies or breathing difficulties are not a concern, smelling a small amount of incense or an unlit scented candle may be ideal. Simply holding either of these items can serve the needs of individuals who benefit from smelling certain fragrances.

- What would church be without bells? Though items that make sounds are not for everyone, a soft bell can be a great source of sensory relief for someone who seeks auditory input.

- Provide palm branches to be touched, carried, and waved on Palm Sunday.

- After the Scripture story, invite the youngest parishioners to find the "lost" (stuffed) sheep that you hid before they arrived. In other words, remember to use wisely the resources you already have.

SENSORY SUPPORT EXPERIENCES

Although there is an enormous selection of tangible manipulatives and sensory items available, there are also many simple interventions that can aid one's ability to be more engaged. You might consider the following:

- Include or increase the age-appropriate opportunities for movement (dance, yoga, acting like a specific animal or character, etc.) and music (if it's not too loud; use noise-canceling headphones if needed).

- Use as much variety as possible. Tracing the letters on sand paper that spell out the vocabulary words or creating doves out of modeling clay engages more of our senses and, in turn, enhances our opportunities for learning. Give permission to remain seated or stand or even to walk around at times.

- Provide a mix of actions that alternate between high, medium, and low levels of stimulation. The more senses we involve in a lesson or prayer, the more likely we are to capture the attention and imagination of more learners.

What is needed for diverse learners is actually good for everyone, adults included. Once you start observing the immediate benefits that take place when sensory-input needs are met, you will want to increase your knowledge and efforts. It is that positive—for everyone involved!

Three Takeaways

- **Creating intentionally designed spaces for individuals with sensory needs not only benefits the person but also helps welcome the entire family to worship together.**

- **Sensory processing is an individualized act, and it's best to provide solutions that most effectively support an individual's preferences.**

- **What is needed for diverse learners is best for everyone—adults included!**

LOOKING AHEAD...

◆ We are all sensory beings. We all have items we crave or resist. What are some of yours?

◆ Which sensory item(s) from the list on the previous pages would you enjoy? Which would you not?

◆ Sensory items can look like toys, but they are tools that greatly assist persons who have sensory-processing disorders. What new sensory items do you hope to incorporate into your space?

✳ NOTES:

_____

_____

_____

_____

_____

_____

_____

CHAPTER 5
Promoting Executive Function and Self-Regulation

BY CHARLEEN KATRA

Getting Started

Where did I put my keys? Why did I come into this room? Have you ever found yourself standing still, asking those questions? Fortunately, in a matter of moments, most of us usually remember what we were looking for. Such scenarios can feel frustrating or even concerning. But for individuals who struggle with memory and other processing skills that we may take for granted, daily life can be frustrating.

TWO-MINUTE CHECK-IN

- What, if any, processing deficits have you observed in your students?

- How have these behaviors been exhibited?

- How have you dealt with these learning difficulties in the past?

Before we explore the processing deficits that some of our students struggle with, let's take a look at the main operating system that governs our ability to pay attention to the minutiae of daily life: the frontal lobe. Often called the "air traffic controller" of our brains, the frontal lobe sorts through a variety of input, enabling us to respond appropriately in given situations. The frontal lobe also works in partnership with other parts of the brain and can affect how easy or difficult life can be. This crucial processor is also the last part of the brain to develop. Thus, some children, youth, and young adults whose frontal lobes haven't fully developed may not yet have the neurological capacity to perform in ways expected by adults.

EIGHT KEY EXECUTIVE FUNCTIONS

Our higher-functioning thoughts, behaviors, and decisions all stem from the frontal lobe. These competencies are foundational for our intellectual and social development and are known as "executive function," a collection of mental skills that enables us to navigate the world safely, productively, and successfully. In this chapter, we will discuss eight key executive functions: **impulse control, emotional control, flexible thinking, working memory, self-monitoring, planning and prioritizing, task initiation,** and **organization.** Though these mental abilities are not in and of themselves visible, our actions can indicate their strengths or weaknesses. An adult with strong executive function skills would likely be described as dependable, confident, and rational; he or she has probably been referred to as a "born leader" or voted "most likely to succeed" at some point in his or her life. Many of our students' executive function skills are still developing, and the good news is that there are effective strategies we can use to help them improve these skills as they grow up.

EXECUTIVE FUNCTION DEVELOPS THROUGHOUT LIFE

Executive function is learned as the brain develops and behavioral skills are honed and improved. Most of us begin acquiring the roots of these skills between the ages of two and six. Executive function skills are refined from early adolescence through young adulthood, and ideally, by adulthood, we've formed a strong mental network—though these skills can still be learned and cultivated later in life. It's never too late.

Once we understand the positive impact of acquiring strong executive function skills, we will also sense how having deficits in these skills can be incredibly detrimental. Not having the skills needed to manage everyday responsibilities can produce significant challenges at home, school, church, or work. Luckily, the more overtly we can teach and offer opportunities to practice these skills, the better.

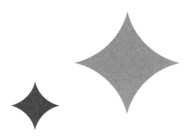

Strategies to Improve Executive Function

Weaknesses in executive function can affect the development of certain mental skills of individuals who have learning and attention difficulties, autism, fetal alcohol syndrome, and other neurological differences. In this chapter, we will examine executive function deficit behaviors, as well as how we can strategically support their improvement. Below is a brief definition of each skill set, a snapshot of how a deficiency may be expressed in the classroom, and suggestions on how to improve proficiency. Some of the strategies may aid the progress of more than one skill set.

IMPULSE CONTROL

Impulse control is the ability to think before taking action, to weigh the pros and cons, and to choose delayed gratification over immediate gratification.

Those who have deficits in impulse control may be risk-takers, engage in dangerous activities, blurt inappropriate things, choose immediate over delayed gratification, or find it difficult to take turns, share, sit still, or stay seated.

Strategies to Improve Impulse Control

- **Interactive games for younger and older students.** Games like "Simon Says," "Red Light, Green Light," or "Mother, May I?" offer opportunities for younger children to practice stopping or pausing a behavior to remain in the game. For older individuals, playing the game "Taboo" helps participants strengthen their inhibit skills by resisting the impulse to say certain words when giving clues. You can easily insert games like this into your catechetical lessons. For example, students could play "Taboo" by using important figures in Scripture. For the Old Testament figure Noah, "Taboo" words could include *ark, animals, two-by-two, flood*, and *raven*. For Moses, words could include *Nile, basket, Egypt, burning bush*, and *Ten Commandments*.

- **Offer incentives for behavior.** State, "When you do [x behavior], then you can do [x reward]." You may need to state this phrase repeatedly. Do so calmly and consistently.

- **Invite students to count down from three in their heads before raising their hands.** There will always be learners who blurt the answer without raising their hands, often the result of a deficit in their impulse-control abilities. Counting down in their heads will help these students become more aware of and hone this skill. You could also give students with impulse-control deficits a sheet of paper with a series of twenty-five rows of three squares each, a copy of which is available on page 177. When they want to participate, invite the students to check three boxes in a row and then raise their hand. Repeating this activity slows the learners down and helps them think before they act. Eventually, they will be able to inhibit the urge to call out and will raise their hand instead. Catechists or teachers can reinforce this behavior by deliberately ignoring the answer of individuals who didn't raise their hands and instead calling on the person who did. They can add, "That would have been a great response if you had . . . . (soliciting the answer, 'raised my hand')," or ask, "What do we need to do before we answer?", then repeat the original question and give the learner a chance to practice raising his or her hand. When they do it well, celebrate!

Want to really stretch learners' inhibit skills? Play "Red Light, Green Light," only with red meaning "go" and green meaning "stop." Double inhibit! Or instruct players to not follow the instructions in "Simon Says."

Now, that's raising the challenge! Love it.

- **Resist the temptation to respond to requests immediately, as long as waiting will not be harmful.** Delaying providing a toy, book, or video game, even briefly, helps learners slow down and grasp the importance of waiting and patience. The act of helping others slow down slows us down too. After all, we all live in the same fast-paced society; pausing and practicing impulse control is beneficial for us all.

- **Add intentional pauses between questions and answers.** Hold up a timer and ask students to wait ten to fifteen seconds after being called on to answer. This waiting forces a pause in the conversation and also creates an opportunity for students to formulate their thoughts more clearly.

EMOTIONAL CONTROL

Emotional control is the ability to appropriately manage feelings to avoid overreacting to situations and stressors.

Those who have deficits in emotional control may overreact, behave explosively, be easily upset, have difficulty accepting disappointment and criticism, and be slow to calm down.

Strategies to Improve Emotional Control

- **Explain the difference between feelings and behaviors.** Everyone gets angry from time to time, but expressing anger aggressively (by shouting and screaming, hitting others, throwing or stealing things) is harmful to the individual and to others.

- **Teach the importance of using words to express feelings of anger, frustration, and disappointment.** When you don't have or know the words to express yourself, you will act out your feelings. You can help learners cope with "big" emotions by using phrases like "I'm mad, sad, angry, or confused." Doing so helps minimize harmful behaviors. Then discuss strategies to help learners return to a peaceful state (talking about the situation, listening to music, or praying).

- **Create a feelings dictionary.** Compile all the words that describe the range of emotions that one might experience. For students who are nonverbal or who are visual learners, include images too, using cards or communication devices. (A sample copy is available on page 178.) The Picture Exchange Communication System (PECS)® and verbal feelings charts (both available online) are great places to start. Having pictures or words to express feelings also helps students understand appropriate behaviors.

- **Discuss how characters in books and movies interact with one another and how they respond in similar situations.** Use the characters to teach about relationships and human interactions. You can then ask learners to brainstorm how they might help others in need.

- **Use words and pictures to describe your own feelings, and model calmness.** When responding to inappropriate behavior, we must always honor the dignity of the person and never correct from a place of anger.

If you have a learner who behaves inappropriately, invite him or her to identify and state his or her feelings. Ask him or her what the appropriate behavior is in the given situation. For nonverbal learners, model the appropriate behavior with picture cards that indicate feelings, or use characters in books or movies to further discuss desired responses. In the end, it's important to show your love and concern and patience. Some students may need more time to calm down before they can express their feelings.

As educators, we can express our own feelings of disappointment by showing the students that we believe in them and that they can do better next time. Sharing our feelings about the incident will also help us connect with students emotionally.

When we connect emotionally with students, everyone will feel more safe, secure, valued, and loved—precisely the type of environment where learning thrives. Look for every opportunity to praise and celebrate what is going right. Be specific, use that person's name, and spotlight him or her.

> When coaching kids on their emotional control, I think it's important to emphasize that anger is not bad or wrong. We just need to learn how to express that we are upset in ways that are appropriate to the situation.

> So important! Jesus provides some great examples too, like the way he responded to the money changers in the temple—and he didn't pull any punches with the Pharisees.

> Hypocrites! Blind guides! Blind fools! When Jesus lost it, it was always about speaking up against injustice.

- **Turn off media and technology whenever possible.** While technology plays a valuable role in teaching, it takes intentionality to build emotional connections and prioritize presence over screen time. Developing emotional connections person-to-person helps us establish and maintain relationships with the people God places in front of us. Remember, we are the most significant realization of God's creation.

FLEXIBLE THINKING

Flexible thinking is the ability or skill of coping with change in a task, game, or schedule and easily adjusting to the unexpected.

Those who have deficits in flexible thinking may be obsessed with a specific topic, be rigid or close-minded in their thinking, and be unable to think of something in a new way.

> Life is constantly surprising us with unforeseen twists and turns. How difficult it must be for our kiddos who have rigidity issues and must deal with this constant flux.

Strategies to Improve Flexible Thinking

- **Discuss real-life situations that call students to react and change course.** For example, you could ask students how they would respond if their cell-phone battery dies, the weather changes, or their car gets a flat tire. Point out that they have choices, and then brainstorm the options they could choose. You can also highlight the choices that will help everyone involved remain as calm as possible.

- **Help students devise their own solutions.** Don't rush to solve a learner's situation. Instead, offer suggestions or discuss possible options while allowing the individual to work out his or her own solution or plan B. Growth in this area, even minimally, will build self-confidence and increase feelings of being in control, which in turn can help lower anxiety and lead to more inner peace.

> I agree! It's important that we teach these students how to adjust to the unexpected. Being flexible also entails learning how to be a critical thinker, freely choosing right over wrong, and being able to respectfully discuss other religious viewpoints. And we can't forget being open to conversion, which is ongoing!

WORKING MEMORY

Working memory is the ability to retain necessary information to use in completing a task or solving a problem. Those with healthy working memory are able to maintain approximately seven items (plus or minus two) for about thirty seconds without rehearsing or reviewing information. Short-term memory is also known as working memory, though short-term memory refers only to the storage of information, not the way it is used.

Those who have deficits in working memory may have poor short-term memory (e.g., not knowing what to do when it's your turn) and trouble remembering instructions even when told multiple times. In any subject matter, we build upon that which we learned before, and memory plays a big part in learning. In faith formation, this can involve memorizing content like the gifts of the Holy Spirit, Scripture verses, and prayers. We can never discount the value of actively using working memory in faith and charitable actions. For example, praying the Stations of the Cross can help maintain the story of Jesus' Passion in working memory, or volunteering by serving food to the homeless builds memories to remember the Corporal Works of Mercy. Making a habit of these sorts of prayers and activities can eventually lead to strong memories linked to faith and action, which will draw individuals back to the Church time and time again.

Strategies to Improve Working Memory

- **Play games that test your students' memory.** For example, place a dozen or more classroom objects—rosary, cross, Bible, pencil, paper—on a flat surface and cover them. Tell participants that they will have only one minute to view the items once they're uncovered. After the minute's over, cover the items again and invite participants to state or write down as many objects as they can remember. Afterward, discuss how they did, and offer strategies on how they can remember more items or names. For example, students could use word association to connect items or bundle similar items together.

- **Play matching games using decks of cards.** Use Animal Rummy, Concentration, and others. For a Catholic version, use holy cards and invite students to match them.

- **Incorporate music and poetry to help students retain information.** Remember how we learned our ABCs? We sang them!

- **Practice remembering a phone number for twenty to thirty seconds, without note-taking.** Then invite students to write the number down and check for accuracy.

- **Play "A Trip to the Market" memory game.** The market game could take place in a small group or a circle. Begin by sharing one item you bought at the grocery store. Invite subsequent participants to recount what was bought before them in the order purchased and then add their additional item. For a Catholic spin, call the game "A Trip to Heaven," and invite participants to state the names of the saints they saw on their visit.

SELF-MONITORING

Self-monitoring is the ability to evaluate progress during or soon after completing a task and modify behaviors accordingly.

Those who have deficits in self-monitoring may be unaware of their actions and the impact on others, not check for mistakes in their work, and be surprised by negative feedback or grades. Strong self-monitoring skills will come in handy when a student takes stock of his or her sins in preparation for the Sacrament of First Penance and Reconciliation or when praying the Examen, a prayer that helps participants review their day alongside God.

Strategies to Improve Self-Monitoring

- **Ask learners to rate their own level of success during and after the completion of a task or activity.** You can also create a checklist with prompts for learners to rate their performance.

- **For learners with autism, use a facial-expression chart.** Learners who have autism often have difficulty reading the facial expressions and body language of others, which makes it harder for them to self-monitor and adjust their behavior in response. Posting a facial-expression chart, a poster with pictures of people's faces experiencing different emotions, can help learners better interpret the reactions of others and then change their own behavior if needed. Start small by using a chart with a minimal number of choices, which is available on page 178, and expand from there.

- **Connect students with "buddies" or peer mentors.** These mentors can help learners discover how to better self-monitor by modeling appropriate behavior.

PLANNING AND PRIORITIZING

Planning and prioritizing is the ability to set a goal and determine the steps needed to accomplish it.

Those who have deficits in planning and prioritizing may procrastinate on assignments and not know what steps to take and in what order to begin. We've mentioned this earlier, but it's worth repeating: We make our plans and so does God. Sometimes our lesson plans get changed. Remembering that God is in charge and all will be well can comfort us all.

Strategies to Improve Planning and Prioritizing

- **For students who experience heightened anxiety in changed plans or routines, place a note at the bottom of a printed agenda for a session or retreat that states "Schedule may change."** This note will serve as a constant reminder that the schedule is flexible. The more we can help prepare someone for unexpected changes (a guest speaker is unable to arrive, there's a fire drill, etc.), the better for everyone.

- **Post the written agenda or instructions in a visible place.** Provide a printed version for those who would benefit from having a copy. Always include the note at the bottom indicating that the schedule could change.

- **Instruct students verbally and in a step-by-step format.** Use as few words as possible and choose words that are simple and concrete—a particularly helpful strategy for students with autism.

- **Have a regular routine and follow it closely.** This will help learners feel comfortable knowing what to expect. Stress and anxiety levels are lowered when the sequence of events is predictable.

- **Ask learners to repeat what you said.** Inviting their response helps check for understanding and underscore what they heard. You can learn more about how to effectively check if students understand in chapter 7.

- **Create a daily checklist with items that can be marked off as completed by the learner.** Besides acting as reminders, checking off steps on the list will add a sense of accomplishment to his or her day.

- **Break down large projects into several smaller ones and provide deadlines for each.** Offer manageable steps that individuals can complete.

- **Design a chart that shows the portions of work needed to complete a project or activity.** Providing a visual schedule makes the totality of steps feel more manageable and less overwhelming. If necessary, you can start prioritizing the list for learners and then advance toward helping them prioritize it on their own. A template for a visual schedule can be found on page 179.

- **Preface the most important information with a prompt.** Prompts could include stating a learner's name before giving instructions or tapping the desk before asking a question.

- **Summarize past information or invite learners to do so before moving on to new material.** This is a good opportunity to check for comprehension. You may also choose to alert learners that the current task is completed and a new task is ahead.

- **Occasionally update students on the time left in class or for an assignment** (three minutes remaining, two minutes remaining, etc.). You can also use a timer so that the remaining time can be seen. (One helpful resource is available at www.TimeTimer.com.) Supporting and promoting time management is invaluable in all stages of life.

TASK INITIATION

Task initiation is the ability to know how to get started independently on a task or activity.

Those who have deficits in task initiation may avoid beginning an assignment and make excuses not to do so.

Strategies to Improve Task Initiation

- **Put on your "thinking cap."** The old children's television show *Back to the Future* used to signal when it was time to begin an activity by saying "Put on your thinking caps." Using words in conjunction with an object is helpful to call attention to or redirect young learners to a task at hand. Start by having learners role-play putting on a cap, either real or imagined. Later, you will only need to say the words "thinking cap" or hold up a cap for them to know that a task is about to begin. Verbal and visual cueing reduces teacher/parent talk and provides a positive prompt that's easy to understand.

- **Offer a fidget to reduce anxiety in beginning a task.** When you're feeling anxious, it can be challenging to get started on a task. Anxiety causes thoughts to wander, and when these thoughts spiral, students are left with too many *what-ifs* to fully concentrate. Self-doubt and confusion can also cause initiation to stall. Having a fidget to hold can be just what a learner needs to relax and better focus. See chapter 4 for a list of recommended fidgets.

- **Incorporate colors, textures, or scents into activities to help capture attention and encourage the desire to get started.** For example, you could invite students to use modeling clay to create a dove for the Holy Spirit, hunt for a stuffed sheep to act out the parable of the lost sheep, or plant flowers while discussing care of creation.

- **Ask a student to identify what's getting in the way of beginning a task.** It could simply be that his pencil needs to be sharpened or that she doesn't have certain supplies.

For some, even initiating small tasks can be difficult. The above tips will help learners gain self-confidence in overcoming task avoidance.

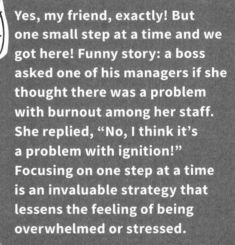

This reminds me of the process of writing a book. 😊

Yes, my friend, exactly! But one small step at a time and we got here! Funny story: a boss asked one of his managers if she thought there was a problem with burnout among her staff. She replied, "No, I think it's a problem with ignition!" Focusing on one step at a time is an invaluable strategy that lessens the feeling of being overwhelmed or stressed.

Guidance and encouragement along the way are very helpful, followed by a completion celebration, of course!

ORGANIZATION

Organization is the ability to keep track of thoughts and belongings.

Those who have deficits in organization may lose track of thoughts or belongings, be scattered when solving problems, and be easily overwhelmed by projects. Keep in mind that there is more organization in our lives than most of us think about. We may think of organization in terms of piles of paper and due dates, but organization also involves the natural order of the world. In the Church, we follow the organization of the liturgical year, which consists of celebrations, hymns, and prayers organized accordingly. We also follow the Order of the Mass, the Liturgy of the Hours, prayers at certain moments in the day, and so on. Are you feeling more organized already?

Strategies to Improve Organization

- **Create a checklist to ensure that all necessary supplies are available for daily or specific tasks.** Prepare ahead of time with learners, dividing busier days or larger tasks into small, manageable units. Create one checklist at a time, as needed.

- **Provide monthly or weekly calendars to ensure that to-do lists remain visible.** Keep calendars in a specific location, creating and updating them with learners. Incorporate checking the calendar into the learners' routine.

- **Color-code items that belong together.** Use different colored tabs in a binder (one color per subject) or use different colored binders or folders in the same fashion.

- **Place a reminder checklist in a personal space** (e.g., a locker, cubby, or closet). Utilize pictures, symbols, or words to indicate important things that the learner is to do, such as greet the teacher, turn in homework, and put away his or her backpack.

- **Create an assignment folder, notebook, or binder that is checked by the educator or parent.** Regular learner/adult communication promotes accountability and supports learners to successfully stay on task.

- **Monitor for fatigue or hunger.** Providing adequate breaks for movement or nourishment supports a learner's ability to focus, which aids organization.

SELF-REGULATION

Another important executive function to note that also affects a person's capability to learn is self-regulation. Self-regulation is the ability to manage feelings and behaviors, and it's also connected with social and emotional development. Beginning in infancy, babies cry, look away, and suck their thumb to manage their emotions. Based on the response to their actions, babies begin to understand cause and effect. Parents, family members, and other care providers become important role models and influence how the child learns to regulate his or her emotions. Children who see adults successfully regulate their own emotions and behaviors will most likely learn to do the same. Vital foundational years for self-regulation skills to be "caught" are from birth to five years of age.

Parents or educators will initially provide maximum support (modeling/reinforcing) during the early years and then gradually withdraw it (only offering cues or prompts) as the learner is better equipped to independently slow down, become calm, make another choice, and self-regulate. Parents will eventually withdraw prompting when the child no longer needs it, and they'll move to monitoring. A child will feel more independent as social and emotional self-regulation continue to develop with age. By grade school, children can often manage multiple feelings and tasks at the same time. The ability to consistently regulate both feelings and behaviors is an essential skill that allows relationships and friendships to be formed and maintained.

SELF-REGULATING WITH ADHD OR AUTISM

Individuals with a diagnosis of ADHD, autism, and other neurological differences can find self-regulation very challenging. They may be unable to concentrate, be uninterested in people or daily activities, become easily upset and worried, and have emotional outbursts that could include spitting and hitting. These behaviors can deter the development of relationships. As educators, we must be sensitive to those whose needs are greater. Each person is unique, and each person will need different levels of support. Approaches discussed in this chapter and others will assist in both supporting and including learners who have deficits in self-regulation.

THE VALUE OF PROMOTING EXECUTIVE FUNCTION

Did you know that promoting executive function competencies in the preschool years is more advantageous to future intellectual and social success than encouraging knowledge of numbers and letters? These critical building blocks are the "how" of learning, while the content of years of coursework is the "what." As with any discipline, these skills take time and practice to develop. You may have already noticed that the strategies discussed in this chapter do not require costly materials. But they do require an investment: a human one, a person or a team of people lifting others up. Simply put, we are all the sum of the interactions we have with those around us.

Three Takeaways

- The behaviors that make up our executive function are skills that can be practiced and developed over time—it's never too late!

- Though mental abilities are not in and of themselves visible, the way they are manifested through our actions can indicate their development.

- It takes time and work to help our students improve their executive function skills, but it's what our faith calls us to do and what others have done for us over the years.

LOOKING AHEAD...

- Which executive function skills are you particularly strong in? Which one(s) challenge you?

- How have you observed executive function skills and behaviors in your students? How have you responded in the past, and what will you do differently going forward?

NOTES:

_____

_____

_____

_____

_____

_____

_____

CHAPTER 6
How to Get and Keep Attention

BY JOHN E. BARONE

Getting Started

Does the following scene sound familiar to you?

TEACHER: "Okay, boys and girls, quiet down now!"(Laughter and talking continue.)

"Class is about to start. Shh . . . Come on, guys." (Laughter and talking continue.) "Seriously, I need you to pay attention. Shhhhhh . . . Please be quiet." (Laughter and talking increase.)

"SHUT UUUUP!" (The class is now silent, with students staring wide-eyed in fear.) "Now that I have your attention, in today's class we will be learning ways we can share God's love with one another."

TWO-MINUTE CHECK-IN

- What techniques do you typically use to bring a group to attention?

- When learners become distracted, how do you perceive the behavior?

- How do you respond when learners are daydreaming?

Maybe you haven't yelled "Shut up," but you've probably wanted to. And if you've taught young people, you've experienced the challenge of getting and keeping students' attention. The frustration and annoyance of constant chatter, interruptions, and tuned-out students can make for a very unpleasant teaching experience. The classroom quickly becomes a battlefield, with the teacher using tools of authority and anger to frighten children into focusing. These aren't our best moments, are they?

HOW DO YOU VIEW INATTENTION?

How we frame inattention makes a huge difference in how we respond to it. Many teachers use a "character frame" for students who are off-task. If instead of attending, students are daydreaming, chatting with other students, or making noise, this is framed as a function of character—the behavior is "disrespectful" and the students are being "rude." How do you feel when someone is being disrespectful or rude to you? Upset, offended, and angry? Think about the impact these feelings have on the lesson, the students, and the teacher. Not a great environment for sharing the faith.

FUNCTIONS OF CHARACTER

The journey out of the character frame starts with reflecting on the motives of the learners: Is the behavior willful? Are students deliberately disregarding the teacher's wishes for them to pay attention? If not, their behavior cannot be a function of character. If it is a function of character, the following scenes would take place regularly:

Scene 1: Deciding to Daydream

Bobby takes his seat, and the class begins. As the teacher is teaching, Bobby thinks to himself, *I know I'm supposed to be paying attention right now, but you know what? I think I'll stare out the window instead and let my mind wander where it will. Here I go.* Bobby stares with a glazed expression and allows his jaw to drop open. He deliberately lets saliva drip from his mouth onto his desk.

Scene 2: Deliberate or Not

Alejandra and Katie are sitting next to each other in the back row, whispering quietly.

ALEJANDRA: "Ewww, Bobby is drooling again!"

KATIE: "That is so gross!"

BOBBY: (Winks and whispers) "I'm daydreaming on purpose to make the teacher mad."

KATIE: "Oh, we should do that too!"

John, do we even want perfectly quiet, attentive students holding on to our every word, unable to tear themselves away to daydream or chat?

Good point, Charleen. It requires enormous ego to think that any one of us who has ever taught should garner that kind of attention, no matter how charismatic we fancy ourselves! Such so-called ideal behavior is really *idealized* behavior.

Exactly! Let's leave room for the Spirit! Sometimes a conversation of great value flows organically from an engaging lesson that will take us where the Spirit intends versus where our lesson plan intended. Or the emotional and spiritual needs of the group may require a plan B (or even C) on a given day. We have a responsibility to lead the group, remembering that God is present in it!

ALEJANDRA: "We're supposed to be paying attention, but let's not!"

KATIE: "Yeah, let's have a private conversation instead. That will really make her mad!" (Katie and Alejandra continue to whisper together, occasionally glancing at the teacher to enjoy her frustration.)

No, no, no. Kids don't decide to daydream. When they get distracted by their thoughts, by things in their environment, or by one another, it's usually not a function of will. They don't choose to have private conversations. They don't choose to get distracted by the proverbial squirrel. It just happens. And for students with attention differences, like ADHD, it happens a lot more often, making them the frequent flyers of teacher scolding. So, it's important to use positive attention-gathering techniques with all students but even more so for those with attention differences in order to prevent them from being labeled (or self-labeled) as "troublemakers."

Scene 3: We're All Daydreamers

Your own experience may be evidence of this too. Do you *choose* to think about your to-do list during the homily, or does it just happen? It happens to me more often than I'd care to admit. Recently, this scene took place at my parish.

PRIEST: (at the ambo giving the homily) "And today we celebrate the feast of St. Catherine of Bologna."

JOHN: (in the pew, drifting off and thinking) *Mmm . . . bologna. I sure would like a bologna sandwich right now. With some mustard, chips, and a nice dill pickle. . . . Mmm . . .*

I didn't willfully choose this daydream. It just happened. And those of you who daydream often know this is true.

Our own experience can help us better understand student behavior. Instead of framing inattention as disrespectful or rude, we need to see it as a developmental difference. Something about these kids' brains makes it difficult for them to stay focused. They can't help it. It's not their choice, and it's not their fault.

John, it's important to remember that learners with attention differences often

- do not pay close attention to details and make careless errors.
- have trouble staying on task and seem not to listen when spoken to directly.
- have trouble getting organized.
- avoid or generally dislike doing things that take mental effort.
- lose things and are easily distracted and forgetful.

Absolutely, and it's essential to recognize that these behaviors aren't willful. It is not due to being rebellious or a lack of understanding or intellect.

Not willful, for sure. Also, not about us. It's not a choice being made to disrupt "our" lesson! Don't take it personally. Best to view it in light of "brain still under construction!" and that this person needs our extra attention and strategies to learn another behavior. More help available on these thoughts later in the book. Stay tuned!

While inattention may have negative consequences for the learner and for the rest of the class, we can't hold the learner accountable in the same way that we can't hold someone culpable of sin if they aren't fully aware and deliberately choosing the negative behavior.

Providing Calm Support

Viewing inattention within a developmental framework takes away the anger and frustration. Do you get mad or frustrated with a learner who uses a wheelchair for not walking into your classroom? Of course not! Imagine that you saw me walk up to a little girl who uses a wheelchair and yell, "HEY! Get with the program and stop refusing to walk, you lazy little girl! Get up out of that chair and walk like the rest of the kids!" Horrible, right? Cruel. Insensitive. Why is it wrong for me to say "Stop refusing to walk"? Because she can't walk. It's a *can't*, not a *won't*. And for many students who struggle with inattention, it's just as much a "can't" as that girl's inability to walk.

When we change how we perceive their behavior, we can become more empowered to calmly support the students in their efforts to attend. Consider Katie and Alejandra, our two students who were chatting during class. Typical character-frame responses include dire warnings of separation: "If you two don't stop talking, I'm going to separate you!" Some teachers wouldn't even give the warning but opt for the common wisdom of splitting the two up as the solution. You may have done so too, and this does make things better in a way. It satisfies the need for a more peaceful, quiet classroom, which is important. But I would argue that a more important value is being sacrificed: the value of helping our learners improve their ability to attend.

An Attention Experiment

Katie and Alejandra were not skilled at sitting with a friend and paying attention at the same time. Since this is something they need to work on, why would we take away their opportunity to practice and improve? Instead of busting them apart, I suggest the following:

TEACHER: (Sees Katie and Alejandra chatting and not paying attention. She approaches, smiling, eyebrows up, and speaks in a very positive tone.) "Ladies, would you like to stay seated next to each other?"

KATIE AND ALEJANDRA: "Yes."

TEACHER: "I'd like that too. And I've noticed that you are often talking with each other instead of paying attention to the class. So, I'm concerned that you may not be learning because of this. Do you think it's possible for you two to sit together and pay attention at the same time?"

KATIE AND ALEJANDRA: "Yes."

TEACHER: "Fantastic. Let's run the experiment and see if you two can improve in this skill."

(The teacher previews, practices, and reviews this experiment with the two girls each time they gather.)

Before Class Check-In

TEACHER: "So, what is your plan for today?"

KATIE: "We're not going to talk during class."

TEACHER: "Good. And what else are you going to do?"

ALEJANDRA: "Pay attention."

TEACHER: "Awesome. Hope it goes well!"

(During the class, the teacher will then track positive behaviors in subtle ways—e.g., a smile with a thumbs-up when they are quiet and focused.)

After Class Review

TEACHER: "How did you do?"

ALEJANDRA: "Great!"

KATIE: "We hardly talked at all!"

TEACHER: "I noticed that, and I am so proud of you! I knew you could do it. Keep up the good work!"

Obviously, this doesn't always work immediately, and sometimes not at all. But, viewing attention as a skill to practice and improve upon ultimately satisfies both values of creating a quiet, peaceful environment and giving students opportunities to grow!

SIGNALS TO GET AND KEEP ATTENTION

So, with a new perspective, let's begin the class again. Your students are gathered and engaged in lively conversation. You need their attention to start the class. With the understanding that they are not supposed to be attentive yet, you gather their attention cheerfully, avoiding techniques that communicate disapproval of their inattention (like shushing or saying "Be quiet!"). Instead, use a signal.

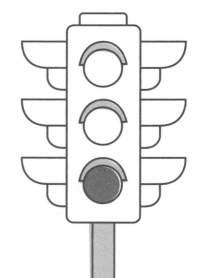

You've experienced signals for attention in your daily life: the ding of the elevator door, the traffic light changing to green, someone waving to you from his or her table at a restaurant. Effective educators teach, practice, and use a variety of verbal, visual, musical, and kinesthetic signals when seeking attention. As you consider which of the following signals to use, be sure to take into consideration any sensory differences or disabilities and provide alternatives. For example, a signal with an auditory component will need a visual aspect as well if you have learners with hearing disabilities.

Using the "God Is Good" Signal

For signals to be effective, they need to be taught and practiced. The teacher will want to first describe the signal and then follow with a practice session. Here is an example of what that would look like.

TEACHER: "Boys and girls, I'd like to introduce a new signal that I'll be using to get your attention. I will say, 'God is good!' Then you will

- stop your conversation and put down anything you are working on.
- look at me.
- say 'All the time!'
- be silent and attentive.

"Okay, let's practice it. You may have a 'blah, blah, blah' conversation with the person next to you."

STUDENTS: (turning to each other) "Blah, blah, blah, blah . . ."

TEACHER: "God is good!"

STUDENTS: (Stop blah-ing and look at the teacher.) "All the time!" (Students then remain silent and attentive.)

TEACHER: "Great job!"

If the students are not successful at responding to the signal, practice again with a "yada, yada, yada" conversation until they get it right.

Teacher Tip: SAMPLE SIGNALS

The best signals are those you cook up with your students, but here are a few popular ones used by teachers to help you get started:

- The sign of the cross
- "Peace" or "I love you" hand signs
- Flickering the lights
- Clap patterns
- Musical instruments, cartoon slide whistle, or buzzer from a board game
- A stopwatch to keep a record of the quickest response time to the signal. Celebrate if students beat the record.

- Song lyrics (For example, using the song "Our God is an Awesome God," the teacher could say "Our God is an awesome God!" and students respond "God reigns from heaven above!")
- Common melodies (For example, using the song "Shave and a Haircut," the teacher could say "Bump badda da duh!" and students respond, "Bump bump!")

Call and Response Signals

Any clever or playful "call and response" combination can be a delightful and effective signal. Here are some examples.

TEACHER: "Hocus pocus!"
STUDENTS: "Everybody focus!"

TEACHER: (clapping) "When your hands are a'clappin'!"
STUDENTS: (clapping) "Your lips can't be flappin'!"

TEACHER: "One, two, three, eyes on me!"
STUDENTS: "One, two, eyes on you!"

TEACHER: "Three, four!"
STUDENTS: "Talk no more!"

TEACHER: "Glory be to the Father and to the Son and to the Holy Spirit."
STUDENTS: "As it was in the beginning, is now and ever shall be, world without end. Amen."

TEACHER: "Meanwhile!"
STUDENTS: "Back at the ranch!"

TEACHER: "Hear ye, hear ye!"
STUDENTS: "All eyes on the king [or queen]!"

TEACHER: "Knock, knock."
STUDENTS: "Who's there?"
TEACHER: "Broken pencil."
STUDENTS: "Broken pencil who?"
TEACHER: "Never mind, it's pointless."

Developing and using a repertoire of age-appropriate, fun, and creative signals will not only improve attention but also bring joy and playfulness to the classroom. It's important to use several and to periodically replace your signals to keep students from getting tired of them.

DOS AND DON'TS FOR GATHERING ATTENTION

After using a signal, it's essential that you begin the lesson only after everyone has responded and you have 100 percent attention. Wait just a few seconds after initiating the signal, and if you still don't have everyone's attention, use other tools to make sure all are attending. Here are some dos and don'ts for attention gathering.

Do

- **Use proximity.** Walking close to those who are not attending will raise their level of awareness and help them attend. It's important when using proximity to casually stroll in the direction of the loudness, continuing to teach and not pointedly looking at the students who are loud. The catechist or teacher just "happens to be in the neighborhood."

- **Narrate progress.** "I have about 85 percent, 90 percent, 95 percent . . . almost there . . . Great, now I have everyone's attention."

- **Celebrate success.** "I see Lisa is ready. Thai is paying attention." Other students will hear this, want some, and attend to get it!

- **Stop using the signal if it doesn't work.** If, after using the signal as well as the appropriate follow-ups, students are still not silent and attending, stop the action and start over. Revert to a loud (but not angry) "Stop!" followed by a calm "You are teaching me that you need practice with this signal. Let me reteach it to you and we can practice." Then go back to the practice step.

Don't

- **Stand there waiting.** The longer you wait, the more frustrated you'll get. Inattentive students often won't see that you're waiting, and kids who are attending may shush the other students to "help" you, making it even noisier.

- **Repeat the signal.** Repeating anything in the classroom teaches kids that they don't have to listen or respond the first time. Repeating weakens the effectiveness of the signal and reduces compliance.

- **Shush.** Making shushing sounds during or after the signal defeats the purpose of using a signal in the first place, and it adds to the noise level.

- **Get angry.** Their lack of response is not willful. Disregard it!

DOS AND DON'TS FOR MAINTAINING ATTENTION

Once you successfully use a signal and have everyone's attention, you can just teach the lesson and enjoy yourself, right? Wrong! General group attention will degrade, sometimes just a few seconds after you get 100 percent. Maintaining attention is essential. Here are some dos and don'ts for attention maintenance.

Do

- **Stop talking.** When students start talking during the lesson, just stop mid sentence and wait patiently. This causes the student talk to be more pronounced and can often restore attention right away. If the talking continues, follow with "Oh, I think I've lost a few folks. Let's wait till we have everyone with us." It's also important to teach your students to do the same when they are speaking. If they don't, gently interrupt with "I'm sorry, but I don't think you have everyone's attention. Let's wait for 100 percent."

- **Use proximity (my favorite tool!).** Often, just walking over to where the distraction/disruption is extinguishes it without loss of teaching time.

- **Vary your volume.** Changing volume, pitch, etc., in either direction does a great job of bringing distracted students back to attention. Remember that a loud voice can lull the same way that a soft one can if it's unchanging. The key is to frequently change the dynamics of the delivery.

- **Deliver a soother.** Just casually walk by the distracted student and place a stress ball or other sensory object on the desk in front of him or her. Most students will immediately pick up the soother and be back in focus with the lesson right away.

> John, let's also point out that some students may already have a personal item that helps them self-soothe. If not, we provide a list of great options to consider in chapter 4, which is on sensory integration.

> Yes, when students have their own personal soothers, they can use them in settings beyond your classroom, which demonstrates more ownership of their sensory needs.

> The catechist would need to approve or prohibit the personal fidget objects to avoid fidget spinners and big stuffed animals, as they can cause more distractions.

> So true! 👍

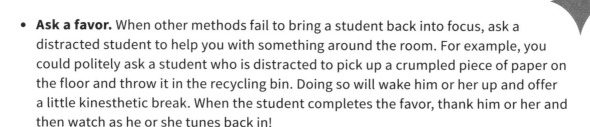

- **Ask a favor.** When other methods fail to bring a student back into focus, ask a distracted student to help you with something around the room. For example, you could politely ask a student who is distracted to pick up a crumpled piece of paper on the floor and throw it in the recycling bin. Doing so will wake him or her up and offer a little kinesthetic break. When the student completes the favor, thank him or her and then watch as he or she tunes back in!

- **Set up a special signal.** Ever notice that when you are in a waiting room, you are often oblivious to other names being called, but when your name is called, you perk up right away? For students who frequently get distracted, you can establish a word or phrase known only to you and the student that you can insert into the teaching to wake him or her up in a way that other students won't pick up on. Be sure, though, that the word or phrase is one that can be easily integrated into normal teaching. *Rutabaga*, for example, would be difficult to integrate naturally! I like to use celebratory exclamations that I normally wouldn't use otherwise. I often say, "Excellent!" or "Fantastic!" but I never say, "Outstanding!" So, when I see the student distracted, I find something in the classroom to celebrate, which is always easy to do. Then I celebrate that success, ending with "Outstanding!" The student hears the secret word, and his or her head pops up like a deer in the forest—tuned in.

Don't

- **Shush students.** As said before, shushing only adds to the noise level.

- **Give them the "teacher eye."** A scowling glance is a negative judgment and is often lost on distracted kids anyway!

- **Overuse a signal.** Signals are perfect for getting attention *before* an activity starts but are not effective to maintain attention in the middle of an activity. Overuse of a signal lessens its potency and can be interpreted as a thinly disguised "Shh!"

- **Call out or correct.** Calling out or correcting a student mid-activity can be embarrassing and reinforces an oppositional stance.

- **Use sarcasm.** Don't use so-called humor at the learner's expense (e.g., "Earth to Johnny!") or insert a child's name into the teaching to wake him or her up, as in: "The Trinity is a great mystery, isn't it, *MARIA*?"

- **Separate kids.** See page 69 for rationale.

PROACTIVE ATTENTION STRATEGIES

Hopefully, the tools provided thus far will be helpful in getting and keeping attention. In addition, here are some proactive ways to improve the overall attention of your learners.

1. Non-Distracting Environment

Take a look at the room's décor and layout. What are some ways you can lessen the distractions in the space? You may want to move brightly colored objects to the back of the room, close the blinds, or lower the shades. Make sure there are places to sit that don't have a distracting view.

2. Alternatives for Seating

Be open to providing preferential seating for young people who focus better in certain parts of the room. The common wisdom of seating easily distracted students in the front is sometimes true, but not always. Look for seats away from distracting views, air-conditioning vents, high-traffic areas, doors, windows, etc.

3. Soother Station

Use a plastic drawer unit to store a variety of sensory objects, including stress balls, putty, and other fidget items. These help students stay focused, expend energy, and reduce their anxiety.

4. Movement

Allow students to move around the room as needed and incorporate kinesthetic activities into your lesson plan.

5. Breaks

Allow group and individual breaks as needed—e.g., walking to the back of the room for a stretch break.

6. Lesson Plan

Use brief, varied activities with frequent movement. Any single activity longer than twenty minutes will increase distractibility. If you have more attention problems than is typical, take a look at your lesson plan and tweak it to make it more fun, exciting, and captivating!

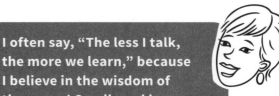

I'd like to jump in with a reminder that we all learn in a variety of ways, so we need to teach in a variety of ways! Aim to incorporate as many of the senses as possible in every lesson. The more engaging the lesson, the more learners stay focused!

Excellent addition, Charleen. And I would also add that although sometimes lecturing can be good, it should be used sparingly, preferably no longer than five minutes or so.

I often say, "The less I talk, the more we learn," because I believe in the wisdom of the group! Small- and large-group work is amazing for empowering ownership in learners and fostering natural peer mentors to emerge among learners, some who will no doubt be future catechists themselves! Let's be great models for them now.

7. Vigilant Monitoring

Students can be distracted throughout an entire lesson without the teacher noticing, especially if they are quiet and not causing a disruption. It is crucial that teachers be vigilant in monitoring students who may have "wandered off" in their minds.

8. Ownership

Teach students to take ownership of their own attention differences and use the strategies included in this chapter—not always waiting for the teacher to intervene.

9. Choices

Offer choices in your lessons to give learners the opportunity to select options that match their affinities and strengths. This will increase their interest level and decrease their distractibility.

TAP INTO THEIR PASSION

When students feel passionate about an activity, they tend to be less distracted and more focused. For example, imagine this phone call from a parent.

PARENT: "Hi, Mr. Barone, thanks for taking my call. We are having a big problem at home with our son, Jeffrey."

MR. BARONE: "Oh, I'm sorry to hear that. What's the problem?"

PARENT: "His ADHD is affecting his ability to stay focused."

MR. BARONE: "When is this happening?"

PARENT: "Mostly when he's playing a video game on his Xbox. He starts off just fine, but then ten minutes later, he gets distracted and wanders off to shoot baskets or clean the garage or some other activity. We can't keep him focused on his video game . . ."

. . . said no parent, ever.

When students are engaged in something they love, their attention difference seems to disappear. So, let's present lessons that they love!

Three Takeaways

- For most students, inattention is not a deliberate choice. Changing the way we frame inattention can decrease our frustration and anger and help us better serve our students.

- Small practices like changing the level of one's voice or using proximity can help students pay better attention. We have many tools at our disposal to make getting and maintaining attention doable for all—and to help students improve in their practice of attending.

- When students are engaged in something they love, their inattention tends to disappear.

LOOKING AHEAD...

◆ What "old-school" tools are you still using that could be replaced: Shushing? Giving learners the "teacher eye"? Correcting? What can you do differently?

◆ How do you view the behavior of learners who aren't paying attention: as a willful disregard of your authority or as a disability they have a difficult time controlling? What can you do to reframe your thinking?

◆ What new attention-gathering techniques will you begin to use in your classroom?

✳ NOTES:

_____

_____

_____

_____

_____

_____

_____

CHAPTER 7

Effective Classroom Communication

BY JOHN E. BARONE

Getting Started

Atypical classroom assignment might sound like this:

"Class, today we are going to do some small-group work. You may choose to be in a group of three, four, or five students. After you've formed your small group, sit in a circle and choose a group leader, recorder, and reporter. Then read pages 5–7 of chapter 4, and take turns discussing reflection questions 1–3 in the blue box on page 8. The group leader will lead the discussion, the recorder will take notes, and then fifteen minutes from now, the reporter will share the group's answers to the reflection questions. You may begin."

Pretty simple, right? Now try this: Cover the instructions above and answer these prompts on a separate sheet of paper:

TWO-MINUTE CHECK-IN

- How would you describe your communication style in the classroom?

- What strategy has worked particularly well for you?

- In what areas of your communication are you hoping to improve?

- How many students will be in each group?

- In what configuration will group members sit?

- What are the titles and functions of each role?

- How will the group roles be decided?

- In what chapter will the small groups be working?

- What pages in the chapter will they read?

- What page are the discussion questions on?

- Which questions will they discuss?

- What color is the box?

- How long does the group have to complete the assignment?

Check your answers by referencing the original instructions. How did you do? Was it tougher than you thought? This level of detail and complexity is not uncommon in classroom instructions—and is very difficult to retain, as your quiz score probably demonstrated! After giving these instructions to a classroom of children, would you feel confident that they understood and would remember what to do in the small-group project?

SIMPLIFYING YOUR COMMUNICATION

Perhaps you've experienced the following scene as a student or as a catechist or teacher when receiving or giving directions:

TEACHER: "Boys and girls, you may take out your books and turn to page 42."

STUDENTS: "What page? What page?"

Usually, more than one student is shouting that question. And this is after a simple two-step instruction! If so many cannot retain two steps, imagine the unknowing that happens in multiple-step instructions. What sort of chaos would ensue after the complex instructions on page 80 were given? Would students' questions and response be framed as "misbehavior"?

For some learners, reducing the number of words and modifiers can help with auditory processing, while for others, the use of visual cues can also increase processing. It's always important to know your audience and their specific needs.

USE FEWER WORDS

Teachers love to talk. Perhaps that's why we are drawn to this role, because we have a captive audience! But the more words we use, the harder it is for students to understand, remember, and follow our instructions—particularly for students with neurological differences whose deficits in processing speeds, attention, and working memory may make it even harder to retain and implement information. So, an important first step in helping our students remember instructions is to reduce the number of words we use when delivering directions. Other benefits of reduced teacher talk include more time for learning, improvement in focus, and an increase in student ownership, leaving learners empowered to take more responsibility in their learning.

Good point!

TEN WAYS TO REDUCE TEACHER TALK

Here are ten easy ways to simplify your communication in the classroom.

1. **Awareness and effort:** Listen to yourself while giving instructions, and become more aware of the amount of verbiage you use. Ask yourself, *How can I say this in fewer words?* You'll be amazed at how many extra, needless words are in your instructions.

2. **Become more comfortable with silence:** Catechists and teachers will sometimes ask a question that students aren't immediately able to answer. After only a few seconds, they'll jump in with a clue, restatement, follow-up question, or encouraging words. Resist the urge to jump in, and allow students time to think—an essential help for including learners who process information more slowly.

3. **Teach by asking instead of telling:** "Spoon feeding in the long run teaches us nothing but the shape of the spoon." —E. M. Forster

   Ask questions that will prompt students to discover the answers instead of spoon-feeding them information. For example, if a student asked, "Why did Jesus cry at Lazarus's tomb?" instead of directly answering, you could say, "How do you think those around Jesus were feeling? How did Mary and Martha react to Jesus arriving late? What would happen when Jesus raised Lazarus from the dead?"

4. **Eliminate echoing:** Try to avoid repeating students' answers. You may find this familiar:

   CATECHIST: Who can tell me the name of Jesus' cousin who prepared the way for Jesus?

   STUDENT: John the Baptist?

   CATECHIST: Correct, it was John the Baptist.

   Echoing a student's answer adds up to a lot of needless teacher talk, and it also steals the thunder of the student who got the right answer. Better to simply respond with an excited "Correct!" and let the student own the success of his or her answer. Some teachers justify echoing by arguing that some students aren't loud or clear enough to be heard. However, other tools are much more effective in increasing student volume, such as walking away from the speaker or asking students to stand when they give an answer.

5. **Encourage cross talk:** In most classrooms, all communication is between the teacher and individual students. In large-group interactions, students rarely look at or address one another. Encourage learners to interact with each other when answering questions or making comments, but be sure to accommodate those with autism or other neurological differences who have trouble making eye contact. If eye contact makes a student more stressed, invite him or her to face the speaker at a safe, conversational distance. You can also meet with the child's parents to ascertain his or her specific needs.

One beautiful by-product of face-to-face formation is being able to witness a community of students working and learning together. That's the Church: relationship building! These communication strategies promote and nurture relationships so well.

Thank you! I think so, too.

6. **Think, pair, share:** Invite students to reflect on an answer to a question and then discuss their thoughts with a partner before sharing their ideas with the rest of the class.

7. **Pass questions:** When a student asks you a question, instead of answering, pass it to the other students by asking, "Who knows the answer to that question?"

8. **Polling techniques:** Use surveys, ranking, continuums, and brainstorming to promote student contributions and interactions. For example, survey students by saying, "Raise your hand if . . ."; use ranking by saying, "On a scale of 1 to 10, how hard is it for you to pray?"; use continuums by inviting students to put a hash mark on a line between "agree" and "disagree"; use brainstorming to encourage student contributions and interactions.

9. **Procedures instead of instruction:** Teach and practice procedures with physical cues rather than with verbal instruction. For example, instead of saying, "Students, you may stand," raise your arms with your palms up to model the action. Physical cues can also be helpful for students with autism and other neurological differences.

10. **Catechists in training:** Provide opportunities for students to shadow you and take over the lesson for a little while. Shadowing works best for activities that don't require prior knowledge, such as inviting a student to help facilitate brainstorming or sharing.

Teacher Tip: "SHRINK THAT INSTRUCTION!"

Practice reducing teacher talk with colleagues by playing a rousing game of "Shrink That Instruction!" Contestants read a typical instruction and then bid on how few words they can use to have students still understand the message. Here's an example of game play:

INSTRUCTION: Children, for our art activity this morning, we are going to take a piece of paper, turn it sideways, and then fold it carefully and neatly in half. After you've completed folding it, fold it in half again to create a little book.

CONTESTANT #1: "I can shrink that instruction to ten words."

CONTESTANT #2: "I can shrink it to six words."

CONTESTANT #1: "Four!"

CONTESTANT #2: "Two!"

CONTESTANT #1: "Shrink that instruction!"

CONTESTANT #2: [Holds up paper] "Do this." [Folds paper as described above]

Imagine how much learning time would be gained if all teacher talk were shrunk as it was above! Read the following instructions and practice shrinking them:

INSTRUCTION: Students, I'd like for you to take out your books and turn to page 32.

INSTRUCTION: Don't forget, ladies and gentlemen, that next week we are going to go on a field trip to serve food to the homeless at the Food Bank.

INSTRUCTION: Boys and girls, for the next five minutes we are going to clean up the classroom. Your job is to push in your chairs, pick up any trash on the floor, gather all of your belongings, and then line up at the door.

Communication Strategies for Giving Clear Instructions

NEVER ASK THESE TWO QUESTIONS

It may surprise you that these same two questions are ones teachers most commonly ask after giving instructions.

"Any questions?"

Most teachers ask "Any questions?" after giving instructions to provide students with the opportunity to think critically and to clear up any misunderstandings about what they are supposed to do. While this may seem like an effective prompt, take a few minutes to reflect on why we may not want to ask students this question.

Perhaps you identified some of the following reasons:

- If students are confused or misunderstand the instructions, they may not know what questions to ask or that they even need to ask a question.

- Some students may be shy or embarrassed that they don't know what to do. They may be too nervous or frightened to raise a hand and ask a question.

- The open-ended "Any questions?" can invite off-topic questions that waste time and take attention away from the task at hand. Some younger children may view this question as an open invitation to ask anything they've been curious about, regardless of its relevance. Sometimes these questions are frivolous, like "What's your favorite color?" while others are difficult to answer, such as "Why do people die?" In addition, because question asking typically peaks at age five, you may be answering their questions for quite some time!

- With older students, "Any questions?" can open the door to their being distracted from the assignment and delaying the lesson intentionally with tangential questions.

The second commonly asked question brings up many of the same issues.

"Does everyone understand?"

Caring teachers want to make sure that all students understand what they're supposed to do. Asking this question gives students the opportunity to affirm that they are aware of the expectations and details of the assignment. While well-intended, is this question the best way to achieve that goal? Again, set the book aside for a few minutes and reflect on why a teacher might not want to ask, "Does everyone understand?"

In your reflection, you may have considered the following:

- Students typically want to please their teacher and may respond *yes* to this question even if the real answer is *no*.
- Students may *think* they understand when they actually don't.
- Students who are confident will respond loudly and clearly, often drowning out those who might be more hesitant or quieter in their response.
- Students may know that they don't understand but are too embarrassed to admit it publicly.
- Students, thoughts are often on the activity, since they just listened to the instructions, and they may not even hear the question.
- Students typically all respond in the affirmative or not at all, so the question may be seen as a rhetorical courtesy rather than an actual query.
- Ultimately, just because a student responds with a "yes" to this question doesn't guarantee that he or she actually understands.

Now that we've identified some of the problems associated with these two questions—and that they fall short as a method of determining whether students know what to do—what can we replace them with? We could just say, "You may begin." But remember the "what page?" scenario from page 81? A number of students won't know what to do, and as a result, they will sit and do nothing, complete the assignment incorrectly, or become disruptive.

We need a different, more dependable tool to find out if students understand the instructions. Keep reading to discover how.

THE CHECK FOR UNDERSTANDING

The only reliable way to find out if students understand the instructions is to ask them to repeat the instructions back to you. Then you will know for certain if they understand. When you administer this "check for understanding," ask learners to list the steps that you spelled out in your initial instructions. Their response will reveal questions and misunderstandings that aren't revealed by the two commonly asked questions.

Take a moment to consider whether the following scenario is a good "check for understanding."

TEACHER: "Students, when I say, 'go,' you may take out a sheet of paper, write your name in the upper right corner, and write down ten things that you are grateful for. Okay, now who can tell me what you are going to do when I say 'go'? (Several hands go up; teacher chooses student.) Yes, Veronica?"

VERONICA: "We're going to take out a sheet of paper, write our name in the top right corner, and make a list of ten things we're thankful for."

TEACHER: "Good job, Veronica!"

While one student clearly understood the assignment, you still don't know if everyone else did too.

Typically, only those who are confident in their understanding of the instructions will raise their hands, leaving those who are unsure to stay quiet and allow other students to list the steps. Learners with slower processing speeds and auditory-processing disorders are even more likely to remain silent. There is no way to know for sure whether students who are not raising their hands are clear on the expectations, which brings us to our next tactic.

The Cold Call

A good check for understanding, then, requires a "cold call," a strategy in which a teacher calls on students who have not volunteered to answer. Did you ever experience cold-call questioning when you were a student? Many of us have horrible memories of teachers putting us on the spot and feeling humiliated when we didn't know the answer. Because of those negative experiences, many teachers are reluctant to cold call.

But without the cold call, you won't be able to truly check for understanding. The key is to make sure that the cold call is safe and doesn't cause stress or embarrassment. Just as you are intentional about respecting the dignity of all learners, make sure to uphold the same level of respect between learners as well. Be especially sensitive to the feelings and participation of diverse learners. On the next page is a sample guide you can use as a model to check for understanding.

A STEP-BY-STEP GUIDE TO CHECK FOR UNDERSTANDING

1. **The Instructions:** Share the instructions loudly, clearly, and slowly, preferably with no more than three steps. Identify each step as step 1, step 2, and step 3, similar to how a phone number is divided up into area code, prefix, and number, which will help students better remember. Never repeat instructions, as this teaches students that they don't have to listen the first (and in some cases, the second and third!) time.

   For example, you could say: "Students, when I say, 'go,' you will do the following steps: Step 1: find a partner. Step 2: sit on the floor with your partner, face-to-face. Step 3: talk with each other for five minutes, sharing ways you have been kind to others this week."

2. **The Approach:** Walk within a few feet of a student. Make sure the room layout gives you access to all students. Avoid narrow rows of desks that block access, particularly for children who are in wheelchairs. Smile, gesture with an open palm toward the student, and ask, "Jonathan, what are the steps?"

3. **The Response:** Watch the student's facial expressions and body language. If the student is not distressed and begins answering, listen carefully to make sure the student understands the three steps. If he is correct, celebrate with a big smile and an affirmation, like "Great remembering!" Then shift to another student. If the student hesitates or shows signs of distress, move on to step four.

4. **The Rescue:** If a student is unresponsive or shows signs of distress, quickly offer two choices: "Would you like some more time to think?" (which is helpful for students who have slower processing speeds) or "You may ask anyone who is silently raising his or her hand for support." If the student chooses more time, wait for the student to recall and share the steps. If the student chooses to ask for support, allow the student to select a peer to share the steps.

   Offering the student this choice helps restore any upset that may have occurred, especially if other students are raising their hands. The option to ask for help or "phone a friend" makes the cold call feel safe. Your students will quickly learn that it's okay not to have the correct answer in your class and that they will not be embarrassed.

5. **Phone a Friend:** After the helper has been chosen, walk to that student and ask for the steps. If the student gets the steps correct, celebrate the learner and then cross back to the original student and ask him to repeat the steps he just heard. If he is able to identify the steps correctly, give him a double dose of celebration to make up for any distress he may have experienced in not knowing.

6. **Celebrating the Understanding:** After getting three or four students to share correct responses, celebrate the group and instruct them to begin following the instructions!

CHECK FOR UNDERSTANDING FAQS

QUESTION: What if a student remembers only one or two of the steps?

ANSWER: Celebrate the part he or she got right and plumb for the rest, offering the "phone a friend" option.

QUESTION: What if the student gets a step wrong?

ANSWER: Again, focus on the positive and offer the "phone a friend" option for the incorrect step. Avoid focusing on the error, and don't use comments like "Oh, you almost got it right!" or "Good try!"

QUESTION: This sounds like it will eat up a lot of class time. Is it worth it?

ANSWER: Teachers should move quickly through the check for understanding (except for during the "more time to think" step) to avoid students' getting frustrated. Also, think of the time as an investment. Consider all the time spent reteaching and redirecting students who are off task or doing the assignment incorrectly when there is no check for understanding.

QUESTION: What if the "phone a friend" helper gets it wrong? May that student phone a friend?

ANSWER: No. To avoid confusion, go straight to the group for the steps when this happens rather than allowing a second helper.

QUESTION: Wouldn't it be a good idea to write the instructions on the board as well?

ANSWER: Absolutely. But because students will experience instances when they receive only verbal instructions or information, it's important to practice retention of auditory instructions.

QUESTION: How can I check for understanding when the learner is nonverbal or has difficulties with auditory processing?

ANSWER: Use nonverbal signals to allow the learner to communicate understanding. For example, the learner could give a thumbs-up if she understands and a shrug with palms up if she does not. You could also write instructions on the board or on an index card, and where appropriate, use electronic communication devices, such as the Picture Exchange Communication System (PECS)®. American Sign Language can be a useful tool as well.

> Another simple, formative assessment technique is to have learners complete and submit an "exit slip" at the end of the lesson. These are forms that students can fill out in response to questions that teachers asked.

> Yes, I like to ask students a summary question and invite them to write their answer on a sticky note to post on the bulletin board as they exit the classroom.

> Right, this helps teachers determine if learners are ready to move on or if reteaching, clarification, or additional practice is needed in the next session.

THE END BENEFITS OF SIMPLIFYING COMMUNICATION

Reducing the number of words we use can make a huge difference in student learning. Learners with ADHD will be able to focus better. Learners with slower processing won't be as likely to fall behind. And learners with less developed working memory will improve in their ability to retain instructions. Talking less may be difficult, but it's certainly worth the effort!

And following up the simple and brief communication with a thorough check for understanding will ensure that you'll end up with a classroom full of on-task students who know exactly what to do!

Three Takeaways

- Deliver steps using few words and communicate steps slowly and clearly in small chunks (three steps as a maximum).

- Do a cold-call check for understanding, allowing students to ask others for assistance if needed.

- After giving instructions, avoid asking "Any questions?" and "Does everyone understand?"

LOOKING AHEAD...

◆ What would you estimate the percentage of teacher talk vs. student talk is in your classroom?

◆ What are some ways you can apply the suggestions in the chapter to reduce the number of words you are using?

◆ Are you up to the challenge of replacing "Any questions?" and "Does everyone understand?" with a good check for understanding?

✳ NOTES:

_____

_____

_____

_____

_____

_____

_____

CHAPTER 8

Peace Be with You: Managing Meltdowns

BY CHARLEEN KATRA

Getting Started

Many of us may have experienced or observed a child's meltdown: the tears, the screams, the flailing body, often brought on by not getting what he or she wants (the candy bar or video game) or being forced to leave a place (the park or birthday party). Meltdowns are hard to watch and even harder to live through. How will it end? When will it end? Who's watching? The situation is made worse when bystanders voice their opinions about an "uncontrolled, bratty child" or a "weak, ineffective adult."

TWO-MINUTE CHECK-IN

- When was the last time you experienced or witnessed a meltdown?

- How did you respond to the child's behavior?

- Looking back, do you feel this was an effective response? What, if anything, would you have done differently?

However, the way in which we view a child's behavior in this situation makes all the difference in how we respond. Most view a child's upset as a tantrum, a reaction that the child can control. However, for children with a disability who have difficulty processing sensory input or regulating their emotions, this behavior is called a meltdown—and it's completely beyond their control. Keeping this in mind, let's learn how to best respond to a child experiencing a meltdown and learn how to help prevent this in the future.

TANTRUMS VS. MELTDOWNS

Behaviors exhibited during tantrums and meltdowns may look the same, but their motivations are different. Simply put, a child experiencing a tantrum can control his or her behavior, whereas in a meltdown, a child cannot. Children having a tantrum can often

- gauge your reaction.
- look out for their own safety and well-being.
- control their behavior.
- communicate their feelings.
- be soothed and feel at peace afterward.

Children having meltdowns aren't purposely trying to disobey, act with rage, or engage in a power struggle. And for the one-in-six children who struggle with sensory-processing disorders, meltdowns often stem from undetected or unresolved processing challenges.

WHAT'S REALLY HAPPENING DURING A MELTDOWN

Individuals who are having meltdowns are unable to control their emotions, and are often experiencing a sensory overload: sounds are too loud, lights are too bright, the air is too cold or hot, scents and odors are too strong, and so on. Each disturbance is happening simultaneously, and the person cannot filter out input or deliberately focus on something else. He or she may respond to such an assault on the senses by screaming, hitting, or running.

Think of these reactions as self-preservation tactics. In times of physical and/or emotional distress, an individual needs to find safety to lessen the pain he or she is feeling. With little to no verbal ability, this desperate need is compounded. Remember the adage "All behavior is communication"? Ask yourself, "What is his or her behavior telling me?"

Imagine not having the ability to ask for help or for someone to turn off the fan, lights, or music. We may never be able to fully appreciate what life is like for nonverbal learners, but consider how you might feel driving a car at night down a narrow street at a high speed as the headlights got dimmer and dimmer. The mere thought of it may make your heart race and breath get shorter. For children who are nonverbal or have other disabilities, this is what living with such high levels of anxiety and charged emotions is like oftentimes.

> At this point, I'm sure some of our readers are concerned about being able to tell the difference between a tantrum and a meltdown. The good news is that the strategies you've laid out for them are effective for both. They don't have to judge. In my experience, imposing the adult's will on a kid is the least effective way to deal with an upset learner—it can turn a tantrum into a meltdown!

> Exactly! Learning about the differences between the two is helpful, but acquiring some positive strategies is what's really important. We'll discuss meltdowns in depth, but here are a couple tips for handling tantrums.
>
> DO: Be firm; help refocus attention; keep the child safe; use visuals; be patient, knowing that "this too shall pass."
>
> DON'T: Give into demands; promise rewards; lose your self-control.

Intervention Strategies to Prevent and Manage Meltdowns

Our goal in this chapter is to present strategies to prevent meltdowns and aid in developing skills to effectively manage them when they occur. Helping an individual who experiences meltdowns requires an understanding of his or her heightened unique world. People who have difficulty regulating their emotions and live with sensory-processing challenges experience the world in stressful extremes every minute of every day. Sensory challenges (discussed in chapter 4) can often lead to meltdowns, so having a variety of sensory fidgets on hand is important—they can be the first defense in helping someone self-regulate and prevent a meltdown. To anticipate or respond to a meltdown, consider these three factors.

1: It's Not About You

In dealing with meltdowns, it's important to note that the behavior is not about you. The sooner we understand this, the sooner we are able to serve as the friend, supporter, and advocate the individual so desperately needs. The individual feels a total loss of self-control during a meltdown, and the experience is always much harder, physically and emotionally, on the individual than on us.

2: Recognize Potential Triggers for Meltdowns

Even before we detect the warning signs that someone needs help, we will want to be aware of his or her potential triggers. Triggers could include the texture of certain clothing or foods or a particular activity. For individuals with intellectual or developmental disabilities and those on the autism spectrum who often experience extreme levels of anxiety, these triggers can make their anxiety levels rise even higher. Another person could prompt a trigger, and sometimes, seemingly nothing could provoke it at all. These potential triggers may seem too vague, so it's best to ask his or her parent or guardian, if not the individual directly, if he or she is able to self-advocate.

3: Detect Warning Signs

There are several strategies we can use to support the individual—methods that we would hope would be used for us or our loved one if the roles were reversed. If we are paying attention, we will begin to see the warning signs, though sometimes subtle, that someone is experiencing social or emotional difficulties. Watch for the following signs:

- Closing eyes, covering ears
- Withdrawing from activities or others
- Refusing to perform the task at hand
- Decreasing ability to engage
- Expressing sounds of urgency
- Further heightened anxiety
- Increasing impulsivity; running away
- Clenching teeth or fists
- Tightening muscles or twitching jaw
- Rocking or hand-flapping ("stimming"), which may help with self-regulation

PREVENTING A MELTDOWN

Think about the resources many of us use to plan our day. We check the weather to decide what we'll wear; we listen to traffic reports to choose the best driving route. What if we took a similar approach to anticipating someone else's day? We could consider what activities are planned for them and how their emotions are faring. Doing so may shed light on what event will pose a challenge or when personal attention or distance could be beneficial. In offering proactive support, we will want to think about ways to provide assistance and redirection sooner rather than later. Considering these strategies before a meltdown will benefit everyone.

Intervention Strategies to Prevent a Meltdown:

- Decrease or eliminate stimulation or an activity.
- Provide choices to lower anxiety and build independence and confidence. Invite learners to choose between a book and a puzzle or headphones and sunglasses.
- Model being peaceful and calm in your presence and voice.
- Praise appropriate behavior and redirect inappropriate behavior to the desired behavior.
- Verbalize feelings on behalf of learners when possible ("I know you're sad because . . .").
- Reinforce verbal information with visual cues. You could state, "It's time to pray," while modeling prayer hands or holding up a picture of prayer hands.
- Post visual weekly and daily schedules.
- Work at the learner's pace and avoid rushing him or her.
- Maintain a routine and advise individual of any expected changes.
- Make activities interesting and achievable.
- Create an environment of mutual trust and respect.
- Provide a safe place within sight where someone can go to cool down.
- Offer fidgets or sensory items for use and permission to access them.
- Create a way to convey his or her feelings when the individual needs a break (sign language, personal signal, etc.).
- Be aware that transitions can be challenging.
- Allow for movement: standing, walking, or moving to a safe place.
- Do not react to behaviors you want to decrease. Instead, observe and respond by redirecting. Offer a sensory item or allow an individual to select one. You can also lead the individual to a safe place for a break.
- Have an established response plan in place, including how to get assistance.
- Develop an emotional-regulation plan to assist the individual with this skill (see page 100 for more details).
- Monitor the student's emotions and plan ahead, as in the traffic and weather example above!

MANAGING A MELTDOWN

At times, there may be little to no advance warning of a meltdown. In that case, how you respond is critical to the person's well-being—socially, emotionally, and spiritually. And the most important, foundational response you can have is to honor and protect that person's dignity at all times. Doing so also models strong advocacy skills to other students who are witnessing the meltdown. Here are a few more strategies to use in managing a meltdown.

Intervention Strategies to Implement During a Meltdown:

- Calculate risk level: does the learner pose a threat to himself or others—e.g., biting, hitting, pushing, grabbing, spitting, or name-calling? Does the student have access to harmful objects that can be thrown or used as a weapon?

- Intervene as soon as possible.

- Maintain a calm composure with nonthreatening body language, such as keeping your arms by your sides with your palms facing up.

- Speak in a steady voice; do not shout.

- Minimize verbal communication.

- Use visual cues such as sign language or pictures to show rather than tell.

- Make sure only one person is speaking at a time.

- Do not threaten to punish the individual.

- Do not make the learner discuss the issue or problem-solve while upset.

- Minimize stimulation.

- Reduce the number of bystanders present.

- Provide ample personal space to the individual. During a meltdown, it's best not to touch the person unless it's necessary to keep him or her or others safe.

- Aim to keep everyone involved safe.

- Attempt to make sure the person does not cause harm to him- or herself, others, or objects.

- Use a pillow or your hand to protect his or her head from banging on floors or walls.

- Be patient. There is a beginning, a middle, and an end to a meltdown.

- Don't take it personally. The behavior is not aimed at you.

- Seek assistance if needed (to reduce bystanders, etc.).

INTERVENING POST-MELTDOWN

No one enjoys a meltdown. They can be frightening, frustrating, and sometimes embarrassing. They are an intense experience for everyone involved. Being responsible for the care of another human being in distress is a monumental task. Please know that feelings of panic, fear, and exhaustion are normal. Once the crisis has passed, it's up to us to help the individual find his or her way back into a regular routine peacefully and with dignity. Getting back on track is the signal that the meltdown is over.

Intervention Strategies to Implement Post-Meltdown:

- Recognize that the behavior is not willful. In this moment, compassion is required, not discipline.

- Allow time for the individual to recompose in a safe place.

- Take a walk together or go outside if possible to redirect the learner to a peaceful state.

- Provide a drink of water using a straw. (The oral motor skill of sucking on a straw may aid concentration or provide comfort, similar to the effects of chewing gum.)

- Don't dwell on what happened. Hit the reset button and start over.

- Offer the individual emotional support. The person may feel sad or remorseful after.

- When the student has calmed down, invite him or her to focus attention on something he or she enjoys.

- Provide verbal and visual calming activities to enjoy, like reading, drawing, or listening to music.

- Maintain good communication with the parent and the parish or school leadership. You want to be an ally, not an adversary.

- Continue to offer support for the individual and his or her family.

- Offer reassurance and prayers for all.

> This is a great list. The post-meltdown care is comparable to how we should act when individuals are injured and taken to the emergency room. We don't criticize or judge them. We just say soothing and encouraging things to bring them comfort after their ordeal.

> I love the hospital analogy! And so does Pope Francis, who has referred to the Church as a field hospital. It made me think of "palliative care." A revised definition of post-meltdown care might be "the pastoral approach to specialized care for people with social and emotional limitations. Care focuses on providing relief from the symptoms, pain, and physical and mental stress of a diagnosis. The goal is to improve quality of life for both the person and their family." Another appropriate and favorite hospital-related adage of mine is "Do no harm."

MAKING UP FOR LOST TIME

Any crisis that causes us to panic will skew our judgment of time. For example, people who have experienced an earthquake may report that it lasted ten minutes when it was actually only two minutes. Meltdowns feel that same way—they feel as if they last longer than they actually do. And many may feel like real emergencies. Fortunately, most meltdowns are not true emergencies in which someone is in real danger; our ability to provide a quiet space and a little time will most effectively help end the meltdown. Immediately following, once everyone is relaxed and regrouped, and while the person is occupied with a calming activity, you will want to adjust the schedule for the time remaining.

THREE STEPS TO HELP LEARNERS SELF-REGULATE

As we strive to instill life skills in our learners that promote social and emotional growth, we will also want to teach strategies that increase their ability to regulate their emotions. Self-regulation is like an internal thermostat in a person. When working properly, it can sense and measure input and compare and contrast information to help the individual choose and perform an appropriate response. Just as setting a thermostat involves intentionality, so does choosing to react without anger or violence. Teaching someone a new skill involves three critical steps: modeling, cueing or prompting, and withdrawing adult support. Think about how a young child learns to eat with utensils or to ride a bike. The child first observes others successfully performing these actions. Then an adult determines the developmentally appropriate time that direct teaching will begin. The adult initially provides full hand-over-hand support (holding the utensil, holding bike handlebars, etc.). As mastery and confidence increase, full adult support is gradually replaced with a limited level of support. The adult may verbally suggest using a utensil or suggest doing so by showing or pointing to a picture of the utensil. Likewise, the adult may hold only one handlebar of the bike and eventually hold only the back of the bike seat. The same process applies when teaching emotional-regulation skills.

Step 1: Model Desired Behaviors

Modeling desired behaviors provides opportunities for learners to observe and mimic what they see and hear others do. When adults are viewed as emotionally calm and peaceful—not angry or judgmental—students will be more apt to focus, learn, and accomplish tasks or mimic appropriate behaviors. In teaching students to regulate emotions, it's important for them to understand feelings as well as have a vocabulary or a means to express those feelings.

- **Offer specific words for feelings (happy, excited, sad, calm, etc.) and connect them to behaviors:** "You shared your book with me. That is being friendly and makes me feel happy."

- **Be intentional:** Say words out loud that accurately describe your feelings or that describe the behaviors you observe: "That puzzle looks difficult, but you are being patient while you look for the right piece. You must be proud that you are being patient." Or, "I am feeling frustrated because I can't find my glasses. I am going to take a deep breath and think about solutions. One solution is to look in my desk. Another solution is to ask someone to help me look."

Step 2: Cue or Prompt Learners

Cueing or prompting is the next level of scaffolding needed to help students self-regulate. To cue a student is to gently remind him to heighten his awareness or initiate action. This offers the student partial support, not total, so that she will eventually be able to self-regulate on her own. When prompting students, be careful not to do the work that they can do themselves. We want to avoid a "learned helplessness," which deprives students of opportunities to grow. For, every time students feel proud of their personal accomplishments and safe in their environment, their stress and anxiety levels will decrease, and this is the foundation and attitude needed for successful learning.

Here are a few ways to cue students.

- **Teach coping skills,** which can be done as simply as saying, "I can see you are frustrated with this activity. You may take a few deep breaths."

- **Encourage the use of self-talk** based on the students' verbal abilities, such as modeling for them the phrase "I can calm down and do this."

- **Lead counting to ten** either forward or backward.

- **Say or hear prayers, or sing,** all viable methods for calming the nervous system.

To help someone change a behavior, we need to teach him or her other ways to respond to situations or experiences that he or she finds stressful. Learning a replacement behavior will help learners cope with their feelings in a positive way. The more a calming method is practiced, the more likely it will become automatic, so that in the heat of the moment, the student will have a tool readily available.

Step 3: Withdraw Adult Support

Pulling back your support is accomplished gradually. Pay close attention to the progression of independent behaviors combined with the developmental level and abilities of the individual. As suitable coping mechanisms are used, providing positive reinforcement is helpful. All learners enjoy being affirmed when they make good choices and are on the right track!

Here are a few ways to create a plan for a student to successfully self-regulate on his or her own.

- Develop it in conjunction with the learner and his or her parent(s).
- Invite the learner to assist in its development when he or she is calm and able to focus.
- Allow the learner to choose support-team members whom he or she finds helpful.
- Identify the person who has the strongest relationship with the learner as the best person to lead the process.
- Regularly review and adjust the plan with the learner and support-team members.

Be sure to consider the following categories when creating a comprehensive plan:

- **Behavioral concerns,** such as losing temper, damaging property, running away, throwing things, etc.
- **Triggers,** such as not understanding the task, being touched or rushed, loud sounds, arguments, etc.
- **Warning signs,** such as rocking, yelling, humming, heavy breathing, red face, wringing hands, etc.
- **Things that improve a situation,** such as drawing, pacing, lying down, jumping, stress balls, etc.
- **Things that make a situation worse,** such as demanding compliance, being touched, teased, ignored, disrespected, etc.

You can also reference the 5-Point Scale, developed by author and special education teacher Kari Dunn Buron, MS, to better understand how various stimuli affect a student's feelings. More information can be found in the Recommended Resources on page 180.

PROMOTING SELF-REGULATION

We are all emotional beings who have good days and bad days. We know that individuals on the autism spectrum often have a difficult time regulating their emotions. Many factors may contribute to this, including neurological differences; a strong, negative affective memory of places, people, or things; difficulty with last-minute changes or surprises; environmental concerns; sensory-integration issues; and societal expectations. All meltdowns are best managed through an awareness of how triggers (lights, sounds, foods, clothing, last-minute changes, disappointments, etc.) can adversely affect an individual with anxiety or sensory issues. Being observant and proactive can help prevent or minimize any negative impact. The combined use of visual schedules, visual timers, transition cues, coping strategies, and established expectations will positively address the cause of the behaviors witnessed during a meltdown. For maximum effectiveness, having these supports in place from the start is best. Lastly, the Participant Information Form on page 172 is another helpful tool to assist you in gathering individualized information to best serve and meet the needs of diverse learners.

YOU ARE NOT ALONE

This chapter has addressed some potentially difficult situations. We hope that you have found practical information and tools to feel assured that, if necessary, you will be able to respond confidently and effectively. Remember that you're not alone. You likely have a co-teacher, "buddies," and parents ready to support you every time you teach. Do communicate to your leadership if additional training, resources, or assistance are needed. Building up the kingdom of God is no small task, but you've got this! Most important, God's right there with you. With this in mind, the most indispensable tools when plans go awry are compassion, understanding, and patience—just what God offers us all.

Three Takeaways

- One cause of meltdowns in children is sensory-integration overload.

- Check with a parent or guardian and, if possible, with the individual, to identify trigger points and warning signs before a meltdown happens.

- Try your best to remain calm during and after a meltdown, and know that the behaviors exhibited are not willful—and not about you.

LOOKING AHEAD...

- ◆ What new strategies will you integrate into your support of learners who have meltdowns?

- ◆ What tools will you use to help learners grow in their ability to self-regulate?

✴ NOTES:

_____

_____

_____

_____

_____

_____

CHAPTER 9
Courtesy Can Be Kryptonite

BY JOHN E. BARONE

Getting Started

Soon after kids utter their first words, parents begin teaching them the importance of good manners, a necessary life skill. Basic courtesy is the foundation upon which all social-coordination skills are built and is a crucial component for success in school and career. Teaching usually begins with "please" and "thank you." Does the following dialogue sound familiar?

> **TODDLER:** "Juice?"
>
> **PARENT:** "What's the magic word?"
>
> **TODDLER:** "Pweeease?"
>
> **PARENT:** "That's right! Here is your juice." (Gives toddler the juice)
>
> **TODDLER:** (Grabs the juice with delight)
>
> **PARENT:** "What do you say?"
>
> **TODDLER:** "Tank you!"

TWO-MINUTE CHECK-IN

- Do you find yourself saying *please* and *thank you* in the classroom?

- How do your students respond to these phrases?

- What are some other courtesy phrases that you think might be effective?

Sweet, right? And so important. But will children learn to use these words if parents and teachers don't model their use frequently? If we don't say *please* and *thank you* often, how can we expect children to do so?

You may find yourself saying, "Please put your bowl in the sink," "Thanks for picking up your Legos," "Please get ready for church now," or "Thanks for sharing your toys with your friend." And as we continue to teach and model good manners and common courtesy, we may notice that there is a cost.

THE REPERCUSSIONS OF SAYING "PLEASE"

Your loss of power is barely noticeable because it's so gradual. But at some point, you may begin to feel your energy eroded from all these pleases and thank-yous. And the adult who was formerly the man or woman of steel senses the presence of that glowing green substance that made Superman as weak as a kitten. Yes, your being courteous with a child can sometimes be Kryptonite!

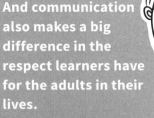

Thanks for this topic! Since the "magic word" in ministry is "love"— and words *do* matter— how we communicate is vital to the respect we show others.

And communication also makes a big difference in the respect learners have for the adults in their lives.

Parents may notice this dwindling power when they find themselves repeating the word *please* to no avail: the bed still may be unmade thirty minutes after they asked to "please make it." By the time they repeat it for the third time, they are practically begging: *"Please make your bed!"*

Who has the power in this scenario? Clearly, the child is determining whether the bed is made or, at best, *when* the bed making will occur. And with each repetition of *please*, the parent's power decreases. The child hears the request, and the word *please* communicates that the task is a *favor* to the parent, making compliance *optional* rather than mandatory. The child thinks, "Maybe I'll make the bed, and maybe I won't!" Usually the volume and angry tone escalate with each repetition, rendering the parent more and more out of control. A yelling, out-of-control parent does not exhibit strength. Children see this behavior as weakness.

Once the child complies with the request, the courteous response is typically, "Thank you for making your bed." In actuality, the subtext is, "You did me a favor by making your bed." Making the bed is a required responsibility. It is not optional. And it's not a favor.

The same is true in school and faith formation. The student is not doing the catechist or teacher a favor by fulfilling a classroom requirement, but we may find ourselves saying similar phrases. For example, have you said the following to a class?

- "Please take out your Bibles."
- "Thank you for completing that assignment."
- "Please break up into small groups."
- "Thank you for turning in your permission slips."

These tasks are all part of students' responsibilities that are expected and required. Using *please* and *thank you* for required responsibilities can blur the lines between a student's job as a member of the class and what is "extra" or "above and beyond." In some cases, such mixed messages can lead children to be more resistant and noncompliant. Particularly for learners who have disabilities that cause rigidity or oppositional behavior, hearing "please" can be a trigger for resistance and argument. If you find yourself repeatedly asking someone to do his or her job, chances are you are saying *please* and *thank you*. But what other option do you have?

THE REPERCUSSIONS OF GIVING COMMANDS

How about just telling learners to do the assignment? Giving orders all the time would certainly not make them feel entitled, but would it impact compliance? Typically, students (and people in general) don't respond well to commands. Nobody likes being ordered to do something, and commanding others doesn't contribute much toward building trust and relationships with young people.

So, if you don't say *please* or *thank you*, and you don't give directives, what can you say? The magic lies in a phrase that has the courtesy of *please* without the danger of entitlement. The phrase communicates obligation without bossing young people around and provoking resistance. And it's nothing short of amazing in its results.

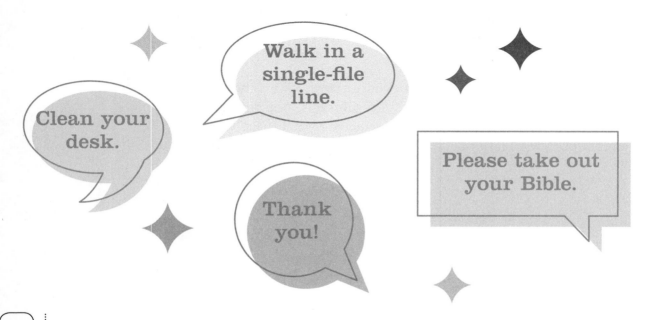

The Adaptive Teacher ➡ Faith-Based Strategies to Reach and Teach Learners with Disabilities

Two Magic Phrases for Compliance

THE FIRST MAGIC PHRASE

"You may." This is a phrase that is simple, elegant, and effective. For instance, you could say, "You may make your bed"; "You may take out your textbooks"; "You may empty the dishwasher"; "You may begin the assignment."

When you use this phrase, you give the child permission to do the task, so you still retain the power. In other words, you're saying, "I permit you to do what you are responsible for doing." The phrase is a cue rather than a request, and the child is typically much more likely to comply than with *please* or another directive.

Increasing the Effectiveness of "You May"

Here are a few ways to increase the effectiveness of *you may*.

- **Offer options when describing a task.** For example, let's say you have a chore you'd like completed, such as taking out the trash. Applying the new phrasing, you would say, "You may take out the trash." This is much more likely to result in compliance than a directive or using *please*. If you want to make it even *more* effective, add a second chore and give permission for the child to choose one of the options to complete: "It's time to clean up the classroom. You may either put away the markers or straighten the desks. Which do you choose?" Adding options gives learners a sense of control over their environment and actions, and they enjoy having the power to decide what they will do next.

- **Offer learners choices of tasks rather than just one when you design and implement lessons.** If you make sure all the choices further the lesson, it won't make any difference which path they choose, and everybody wins! We all love the freedom of getting to decide what we do. By providing them options, you will find that learners will be much more likely to comply with our prompts than when we give them just one task to accomplish.

> But if you tell teenagers "You may," they can respond with, "I may? Well, then, I also may not!"

> Good point. I've been using this phrase for many years, and there have been a few times when teens have responded this way. Usually it's more about making a joke than resisting my request. What I like to keep in mind is to not let them push my buttons and to make it implicit in my tone that if they don't comply, there will be a consequence.

- **Add an enticement.** Making it clear to learners that an enjoyable activity is conditional on whether they complete a desired task is especially effective for learners with disabilities that may contribute to noncompliance. So, consider changing "You may complete your chapter review" to "When your chapter review is completed, you may play Scripture charades with your friends." This gives learners control of their actions and the resulting consequences and has the added benefit of reinforcing a "first work, then play" ethic.

After the individual complies, what do you say to replace *thank you*? Nothing at all? You could, but then you'd miss the opportunity to celebrate the person's success. You want to positively reinforce the completion of the task, but at the same time, you don't want to entitle.

THE SECOND MAGIC PHRASE

"Great job!" As in, "Great job making your bed!" "Great job on your small-group presentation!" "Great job completing your project on time!"

"Great job!" celebrates the child's completion of the expected task, and it also reinforces the child's desire to complete future tasks as a result of the praise. Saying so does not communicate that the task was a favor or personally benefited the adult in any way. The phrase is an objective observation, evaluation, and celebration without the entitling effects of "thank you."

A word of caution: you will not want to overuse this phrase and thus weaken its impact. Instead, substitute other celebratory phrases such as "Awesome work!" "Terrific achievement!" or "Fantastic progress!" Adding specifics enhances the impact of the celebration. Make sure you specifically address what the child did that was worthy of celebrating. For example, if the child's responsibility was to remember to put the Bibles away and he or she was successful, say "Great job remembering!" or "Great job putting the Bibles away!" These phrases better reinforce a child's follow-through than a general "Great job!"

Most of us remember what Charlie Brown's teacher sounded like. For some children, adult voices can sound similar quickly. The two phrases you've shared do work! They also remind me of our desire to use fewer words and, more important, to choose our words wisely. For children with little vocabulary, holding up a textbook, Bible, or rosary can indicate what's happening next or what they "may do." And holding up a thumbs-up sign can be a nonverbal way to say "Great job!"

Good suggestions. Procedures that are a regular part of the routine need no words at all, just an agreed-upon signal!

THE DANGER OF ASKING "OKAY?"

Many teachers and parents have developed a habit of adding "okay?" to the end of their instructions. This phrase is another communication style that can entitle learners. For example, you may say, "Please pack your backpack for school tomorrow, okay?" "Everyone, take your seats now, okay?" "Be on your best behavior at Mass this afternoon, okay?" "I'd like for you to finish the assignment by Monday, okay?"

Adding "okay?" to instructions seeks permission *from the child* instead of giving *the child* permission—which is equivalent to prefacing all instructions with "Is it okay with you if . . ." Doing so can set a standard for learners that they have the final approval over tasks instead of the parent, teacher, or catechist.

CAN YOU EVER SAY "PLEASE," "THANK YOU," OR "OKAY"?

You absolutely can, just not for instances that are the expected responsibility of the child. For example, use *please* and *thank you* only when learners are being asked to do you a favor or something they are not personally responsible for. And *okay?* is appropriate if the request is optional. This way, you can model good manners without creating a power imbalance or a sense of entitlement.

Following are a few examples of the appropriate use of *please*, *thank you*, and *okay?*:

- "Janet, would you please help Pablo, our new student, find his way around campus today?"

  Janet's job is not to orient new students, and she would be doing you a favor by helping him. So, it's appropriate for you to say *please*.

- "Thank you for helping collect the homework assignments."

  There is no expectation that one student collects the other students' work to turn in. This student is doing you a favor by helping with the task, so the use of *thank you* is perfect here.

- "It's such a beautiful day. Let's sit outside, okay?"

  Sitting outside is not obligatory, so the use of *okay?* is appropriate.

SMALL CHANGES, BIG IMPACT

These seemingly minor changes to language can have a dramatic impact on power dynamics. In my experience, adults who have made the commitment to use *please*, *thank you*, and *okay?* only for favors or options have noticed a significant increase in compliance and cooperation and have experienced much less resistance and opposition to requests.

Using *please* and *thank you* just for favors has the added benefit of increasing the potency when you do use these expressions. Hearing them only in the context of personal favors makes them more meaningful to the child. They really feel the extent of your gratitude when it's not offered for virtually every breath they take!

Furthermore, teachers who have consistently used *you may* for student responsibility prompts typically see and feel a dramatic improvement in their authority and control of the classroom. Every time a teacher uses *you may*, the assumption that the teacher has the final say in what happens in the classroom is reinforced. This results in students feeling more secure and more open to teacher guidance and a profound reduction in their feelings of entitlement and freedom to disregard the "requests" of the teacher.

Consistently using *great job* and other similar affirmations to celebrate student successes also has a transformative effect on the classroom milieu. *Great job* communicates that the student achieved something worthwhile. It is also a communal celebration, which creates a climate of appreciation and positive affirmation. You'll soon see students observing the successes of their peers and celebrating one another. Great job!

The Adaptive Teacher ➡ Faith-Based Strategies to Reach and Teach Learners with Disabilities

OLD HABITS DIE HARD

If you decide to make these changes, know that they are not easy, especially for those of us who have decades of teaching experience. Asking us to not say *please* and *thank you* is like asking us not to breathe. (Especially for us Southerners who love our hospitality!) And if you've developed a habit of adding *okay?* to the end of all your instructions, it will continue to come out of your mouth before you even think about it. "You may" and "Great job" may feel awkward at first, but after multiple repetitions, it will be as automatic as "please" and "thank you." Here are a few tips to help you adjust to this new phrasing.

- **Be patient with yourself.** The first step is awareness. You will be surprised when you become more aware of how often you use these expressions. Begin by slowly working at integrating the alternatives. You'll continue for a while to sometimes use them inappropriately, but eventually you'll find yourself saying "You may" and "Great job" more than the other expressions. And as compliance increases and entitlement decreases, you'll be even more motivated to continue working to change your communication.

- **This new phrasing will be new to learners, too.** The first few times you say "You may," it might be confusing for students. It may be helpful to be transparent, sharing that you are trying new ways to communicate with them and that you won't be using *please* and *thank you* for things that are not favors. This transparency will help learners understand the changes, but don't be surprised if one of your students quips, "You may collect our homework now. And great job on the lesson today!"

After making these changes, you may begin to see more success with your students. Ultimately, you'll use these expressions correctly without thinking about them, fully integrating the new vocabulary usage and reaping the benefits.

Three Takeaways

- While using phrases like *please* and *thank you* may seem courteous and a model of good manners, they can actually be an ineffective mode of communication that takes power away from a parent or an educator.

- Using phrases like *you may* results in less entitlement and more compliance.

- Becoming more aware of the language you use will help all thrive in the learning environment.

LOOKING AHEAD...

◆ What tasks do you often say *please* and *thank you* for that are really the learner's responsibility?

◆ Try replacing these phrases with *you may* and *great job*. Do you notice a difference?

◆ Do you ask "okay?" after giving instructions? What could help you remember not to use that expression in the future?

✳ NOTES:

_____

_____

_____

_____

_____

_____

_____

CHAPTER 10

Becoming Lifelong Learners: No Stickers Required

BY CHARLEEN KATRA

Getting Started

You may remember the tsunami of excitement that Oprah Winfrey created every time she announced, "You get a car! And you get a car!" or some other prize just for being at her studio that day. In recent decades, this practice of handing out prizes has also trickled into the classroom. Many of us may give out awards and trophies to children and youth just for participation, making everyone feel like a winner.

TWO-MINUTE CHECK-IN

- **What rewards do you currently offer your students?**

- **How do your learners respond to these rewards?**

- **What intangible rewards might you offer your students instead?**

Looking back over the years, we can see that this practice wasn't always the case: many generations grew up with the adage "Spare the rod, spoil the child." Was that ideology too harsh? Did it form capable and confident adults? Or have years of adulations and self-celebration formed individuals that are less motivated to learn or work independently? Has one method proven to be more effective?

THE TRUTH ABOUT REWARDING LEARNERS

In the classroom, giving out rewards to learners takes less time and effort to implement than fostering internal motivation in them and can quickly become a rote means of classroom management. Though many educators believe that rewarding students is a helpful motivator for learning, in truth, there are far more effective means. For, often enough, the reward is used as a carrot for compliance. In the end, the only person motivated by the encounter is the one dangling the carrot; the reward may produce the desired behavior but not a lasting one. If the learner feels no ownership or innate desire to continue the positive behavior, he or she will likely behave this way temporarily, at best.

The biggest danger is when rewards are contractual: if you draw a picture of a giraffe in pre-K, you'll get a sticker. If you get three A's on your report card, you'll get $5 per A. If you graduate from high school with a GPA over 3.5, you'll get a car. Growing up with contractual agreements like these can result in a learner growing up with a relatively low level of moral development: "If I do the right thing, I'll get rewarded for it." If we want individuals to do the right thing because it's the right thing, we must find other ways to get them to do so than bribes. There may be many times when the same achievement gets no reward at all, other than our joyful praise!

MOVING FROM EXTERNAL REWARDS TO INTERNAL REWARDS

One of the biggest detriments of an extrinsic reward system, in which learners only receive outside motivation, is that learners' innate and amazing gifts risk going unseen and underappreciated. Making this shift away from external rewards is particularly important for diverse learners who likewise seek and deserve recognition for abilities that may be beyond social or academic achievements. In the following paragraphs, we will discuss new behaviors and classroom-management styles that will help your students be motivated and thrive throughout life, in educational and social settings.

Step 1: Pinpoint and Nurture Your Learners' Talents

Although our hearts are in the right place, identifying and nurturing our learners' talents and passions would be a more rewarding use of time spent together. Think about the things you are naturally good at and enjoy doing. Do you need someone to motivate you to read, paint, garden, sing, travel, cook, or write? Probably not, because your motivation is coming from within, from a place of deep desire and enjoyment. This is called an intrinsic reward system, when no artificial or outside motivation is required. Ask parents or educators if they want their children or students to grow up to be dependent or independent, and they will likely resoundingly say, "Independent, of course!" Why, then, do we frequently and collectively interact with young people in ways that hinder rather than help them reach this goal? Are there better ways to instill independence? By respecting and celebrating the unique gifts and authentic accomplishments of individuals, we will more aptly instill in them feelings of independence and self-worth.

It takes time to get to know the individuals you teach. When you do so, you'll discover where their passion lies and what interests them. And once you know their interests, you will become their ally. Even the youngest students can sense your genuine interest in them. To find out more about your students, invite them to fill out the Getting to Know Me form on page 170 in the back of the book. Doing so will help you incorporate their favorite topics into your lessons or activities and help you make connections to their world that will naturally lead to interested and self-motivated participation. When learners are engaged, the need for behavior-management strategies, stickers, or other tangible rewards will often decline or disappear.

Yes, yes, yes! It's easier to captivate than to control!

And a lot more fun for everyone involved too!

As educators, we must help learners identify their strengths and remind them when they forget. Many of us can make a long list of our weaknesses but struggle to identify even a few of our strengths. To nurture and motivate someone's personal growth, we need to continually affirm appropriate behaviors as often as we observe them—from staying on task to being patient, creative, empathetic, and kind. We must also recognize that many students are blessed with gifts and talents that are less visible. Not everyone will excel at visible talents such as playing instruments or sports, but many have less obvious talents that are just as beneficial and a blessing to the individual and those around him or her. Look for and praise intangible gifts whenever they're exhibited: kindness, patience, forgiveness, love, etc. And celebrating someone for being present is fine too! Some would say that no life skill blesses the world more than having a kind and generous heart. We want to celebrate all the tangible and intangible gifts from God that are present in our learners.

Step 2: Make Your Learners Feel Seen

Acknowledging someone's presence—even stating his or her name when that person arrives or leaves—has the power to make a learner feel seen. When someone feels seen, that person becomes visible, and there is value and dignity in being made visible. As educators, we hope to make all our learners feel visible and emphasize their strengths while also helping to improve their weaknesses in a caring and safe environment. You probably remember an educator who left an impression so strong that you have remembered his or her impact for years since. Maybe that teacher acknowledged or appreciated your gifts, leaving a handwritten note sharing what she admired or words of encouragement. Reaching into our students' hearts, nurturing and identifying their talents, and encouraging them offers them this same long-lasting gift. How do you think individual learners might feel if they saw a large note written on the board that called them by name and described how much they were valued as a member of the group? They would probably never forget that moment either.

The parable of the sower and the seed offers a helpful analogy on what different learning environments can produce. Warm and caring learning environments provide a joyful place where everyone is appreciated and encouraged to succeed. Educators (the sowers) need to be dedicated to the hard work of teaching (planting seeds), while recognizing the effects that the environment and climate also have on the soil (their learners). Add a safe and supportive climate that offers an organized schedule with room for adaptations and modifications as needed, and you can be sure of having a very successful harvest. All learners have gifts, and each person's gifts add to the bounty of the entire group. We are all blessed by one another's presence and God-given talents.

MOTIVATING YOUR LEARNERS WITHOUT REWARDS

Our goal is to guide learners to a place where intrinsic motivation leads to learning—and not to rely on or use rewards. Have you ever used rewards to motivate a family pet to perform a certain behavior? This may work for the pet, but in an educational setting, it's much more beneficial to foster hard work and dedication, skills that will serve learners well their entire lives.

And when we do award high achievers, we need to keep in mind that this often leads to the exclusion of rewards for others, which, in the end, hinders our desire to build a strong community of believers. We need to broaden our scope of recognition to more accurately reflect our values. As educators in faith communities, we want to emphasize the importance of building relationships, celebrating diversity, and forming happy, healthy individuals who know they belong and are loved in this world for who they are—gifts from God.

> I feel strongly that learners' belief in their ability comes mostly from achievement. It's great to celebrate the success of the kids we work with, and you know I believe in that 100%, but if all we do is tell them how wonderful they are, it will result in entitlement and a false sense of self rather than growth in self-esteem and high motivation. Coaching them in taking ownership of their own development will lead to growth in their intrinsic motivation to continue to learn!

In his article "The Risk of Rewards," author Alfie Kohn writes, "In short, good values have to be grown from the inside out. Attempts to short-circuit this process by dangling rewards in front of children are at best ineffective, and at worst counterproductive. Children are likely to become enthusiastic, lifelong learners as a result of being provided with an engaging curriculum; a safe, caring community in which to discover and create; and a significant degree of choice about what (and how and why) they are learning. Rewards—like punishments—are unnecessary when these things are present, and are ultimately destructive in any case."

> So true. We want all learning to be transferrable to the future. Motivation that comes from within remains within; everything else is fleeting!

When we move beyond giving superficial stickers as motivational tools to seeing every person as the potential learner that he or she is, we will more likely be enthused to motivate and encourage growth. The more we exhibit a hopeful attitude about learning, the more others will do the same. We always want to improve our learners' belief in their ability to complete a task or learn a new skill.

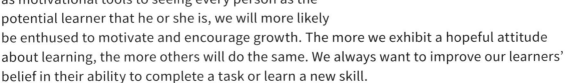

The Importance of Equal Investment in Learning

In learner-centered educational settings, learners are self-motivated and work hard alongside their teachers. Both parties are invested in the joy of learning and in helping everyone succeed. Choices are provided that support individualization and differentiated instruction.

For example, think back to when you were a child about to leave the house on a rainy day. You were probably told to put on your raincoat and boots and get an umbrella. And you may not have given it another thought. You did what you were told to do, and for many of us, that continued for years. What if someone sat alongside us on that rainy day and asked what we saw out the window, what the weather was like, what we thought we should wear or bring with us outside? Even if we planned wrong, we would still have learned an important lesson. Either way, someone would have believed in our ability to think critically, analyze data, and problem-solve, and as a result, our confidence and self-esteem would have been boosted. What a difference this style would make in the classroom.

Teachers have an obligation to share their knowledge with learners, but not at the expense of withholding personal-growth opportunities from them. When teachers do all the talking and deciding, motivation to learn and self-confidence decrease while dependency increases. Even though abilities may vary greatly among learners, every learner deserves the same respectful collaborative approach. Here are a few ways to apply a learner-centered approach in the classroom.

- Pose a question and ask students to answer instead of providing all the information, boosting their critical-thinking skills.

- Allow learners to work in dyads or triads to build community and tap into shared/group wisdom.

- Offer different activities for learners to choose from that all teach the same concept, allowing learners to choose the one that best matches their learning style.

Advancing to a learner-centered approach from a teacher-centered one is a major shift. It may feel like a loss of control, which may be why many struggle to move forward in this approach. Be assured that the fulfillment you feel will quickly make you a believer and likely a happier educator.

REFLECT GOSPEL VALUES

According to every gospel value we profess, love is unconditional. We are called to live out that value in our educational settings too. When our expectations are too lofty for some learners, and only the best and the brightest are celebrated, we are teaching that love is conditional. In response, learners will feel secure and valued only when they are recognized as being the most accomplished [fill in the blank]. No matter how successful a student later becomes, his or her motivation is often driven by a need to please others. And sometimes, a learner can lose the ability to find joy or pleasure in even his or her brightest accomplishments. Likewise, learners who don't receive praise for their best efforts can feel defeated and simply give up or, worse, feel unloved or angry, leading to bouts of depression or acting out. Either way, this method often results in a stunted development. If we as parents, educators, or role models do not shine a light on students' inner gifts, they will remain hidden even from themselves. We all want someone to recognize our uniqueness and not compare us to others.

RESPOND INSTEAD OF REACT

Every human being will make mistakes or less-than-ideal decisions from time to time, regardless of his or her age or ability. Learners who have poor social skills or emotional or behavioral disabilities are no different. As teachers, we have an excellent opportunity to model and teach good decision making. And our method of managing those in our care is directly connected to how well we do or do not influence students to develop decision-making skills. When we respond punitively to misbehavior, we don't allow students to learn how to change their behavior in the future. And how will learners grow to become good decision makers if we don't teach them to practice this art? When we react defensively to learners who are playing around or misusing items, we send the message that they do not have the capacity to improve or make a better choice for themselves. We also send a message that is inconsistent with the faith we profess. Imagine if God responded similarly to us when we snap at someone or have a "holier than thou" moment. Fortunately, God always offers us mercy and forgiveness! Consider the following prayer:

> Father, In your love you have brought us
> from evil to good and from misery to happiness.
> Through your blessings
> give the courage of perseverance
> to those you have called and justified by faith.
> Grant this through Christ our Lord. Amen.
>
> —*Rite of Penance,* Concluding Prayers

It's important that we bless others as we ourselves have been blessed. The learners who challenge us the most are not doing so on purpose. They need our pastoral care—their behaviors tell us so! When we respond in a noncombative stance, individuals receive a message that we sincerely desire to teach them how to self-correct any missteps. Of course, we ourselves are trying to learn a new behavior, so responding versus reacting may seem counterintuitive. Instead of separating learners who continue talking to each other, invite them to state the expected behavior (check for understanding), and then allow them to own the decision to practice making better choices so they can remain sitting near each other.

Some of the ineffectiveness of the reward system is brought on by our attempts to curtail human traits, some of which are quite positive, such as creativity and joy. These two "talents" have no doubt gotten many a learner on the receiving end of disciplinary actions. If we feel the need to bribe or offer tangible rewards to achieve expected behaviors, then we may need to rethink the desired behaviors and the real cost to the learner. We might ask ourselves if our actions are causing more problems than we intended to avoid.

SET CLEAR EXPECTATIONS

Being clear about expected behaviors is necessary, followed by consistency. Some possible behavioral expectations are

- practicing active listening, not speaking when someone else is,
- being cheerleaders/advocates for all members of the learning community, supporting and affirming each other at all times and not teasing or laughing at anyone, and
- prioritizing and self-monitoring the number of questions and comments raised, being aware that others may also want to participate and that some individuals require more time to process and express their thoughts.

Learners who are held accountable are allowed—even encouraged—to remain in situations that challenge them to make better choices. Such opportunities, even in the earliest social and academic settings, instill the ability to develop good decision-making skills and to act in ways that benefit the greater good. These are behaviors that will not only bless the individual throughout his or her life but will also be a blessing to the entire world. We never want to do a disservice to someone by removing potential learning opportunities. When we hold learners to higher standards, we teach discernment skills and the values of patience, generosity, understanding, and empathy.

SIMPLE STRATEGIES TO REINFORCE POSITIVE BEHAVIOR

Learners of all ages inevitably seek positive reinforcement and approval. Here are a few ways to reinforce positive behavior that are easy to implement without any financial cost to you.

- **Publicly praise learners who are on task.** Learners who are not being praised will naturally desire to receive the same affirmation, which will encourage them to re-think their behavior and make necessary adjustments.
- **Allow learners to listen to music during certain projects.** They may also participate in a dance contest or read as a reward for appropriate behavior.
- **Acknowledge the whole group.** This way, diverse learners are also included and

feel a sense of belonging, while other learners may be influenced by peer pressure to perform well. Every time you praise one person or a group, invite that individual to place a marble in a clear jar, which will serve as a great visual marker of praise reports. We want to encourage everyone to notice and celebrate positive behaviors that happen in a learning environment.

- **Make "sunshine" calls.** Let's face it: most parents receive calls only when something negative needs to be discussed. Sunshine calls are made to let parents know how well their son or daughter is doing, advise them of their child's tangible and intangible gifts, and share how you enjoy teaching their child. Imagine the joy in a family's home after such a call. How fast do you think the practice of this "good news" would spread among parents and learners? Sunshine calls are an excellent way to maintain positive relationships with parents and motivate learners who will want their parents to receive a call. Make sure to keep track of these calls so that all learners' parents eventually receive a call and some families don't receive more than one.

- **Invite learners to mentor others, either peers or younger learners.** Mentorship will not only affirm an individual's talents and abilities but could also inspire him or her to seek out a teaching career in the future! Either way, mentoring others will enhance the individual's feelings of self-esteem.

> I love the "sunshine" call technique, but I want to warn readers that the first time they call may result in a parent jumping to conclusions and asking, "What did he do now?!" 😄

> Exactly! Because most parents never get such a call. I hope some do now!

THE LONG-TERM REWARDS

If we never offered stickers, trophies, and other material rewards from the start, no one would expect them, and they wouldn't be missed at all. What every learner deserves is to belong to the community, to be treated with dignity, and to be recognized and valued for his or her God-given gifts. These desires are exactly what their parents want for them as well. When we authentically encourage learners and inspire curiosity and a passion for knowledge, we are more likely to obtain our biggest reward (though we may not be there when it comes to fruition): those we are blessed to teach acquiring the ultimate personal gift of becoming lifelong learners. That is, learners who want to learn simply for learning's sake, no stickers required.

Three Takeaways

- **Offering learners physical rewards may seem like an easy and effective practice, but in reality, this method only briefly motivates individuals, providing little to no long-term learning.**

- **Identifying and nurturing a learner's gifts and making him or her feel seen will have fruitful and lasting effects.**

- **Setting clear expectations for behavior and then reinforcing this behavior will help instill the gifts of lifelong learning and curiosity in young people.**

LOOKING AHEAD...

◆ When learners are engaged, what impact does this have on the need for behavior-management strategies?

◆ What are some tangible or intangible gifts and talents that you can affirm in your learners?

◆ Which parents will be the first to receive "sunshine" calls from you?

✳ **NOTES:**

_____

_____

_____

_____

_____

_____

CHAPTER 11

Can You Relate: Building Connections with Learners

Getting Started

In seventh grade, I was infamous for my smart-aleck comments in class, much to the delight of my classmates and chagrin of my teachers. In my mind, I was a savvy truth teller, cutting to the heart of the matter. To adults, I was immature and a pain in the neck.

The middle school teachers tried everything: they gave me low-conduct grades; I saw them as a badge of honor. They separated me from my most ardent supporters; I got louder to reach my biggest fans. They sent me to the principal's office; I heard the cheers from my classmates in nearby classrooms as I walked down the hall.

Nothing worked. Until Sister Elizabeth came up with a brilliant plan. After one of my more sophomoric comments, Sister asked me to stay after class to talk.

The classroom "Ooh-ed!" making it clear that she was outmatched. I wondered what kind of scheme she had concocted to take down the class clown. Was she doomed to fail like all the others?

Sister waited till the other students left the room and then turned to face me. She looked me square in the eye and asked, "Do you like to bowl?"

TWO-MINUTE CHECK-IN

- How have you dealt with misbehavior in your classroom?

- Do you remember a time when you were successful turning a student's behavior around? When was a time that you weren't?

- What tactics have worked well in forming successful relationships with your students?

I didn't see that coming. I was momentarily stunned.

"Um . . . sure."

"Well, I do too, and I'm looking for a bowling partner. Do you think we could meet at the bowling alley every Thursday after school to bowl a few games?"

"I—I guess."

"Great!"

From that point on, we met every Thursday. We bowled. We laughed. We got to know each other. I learned that she was a Cincinnati Reds fan just like me. She taught me how to use the arrows on the lane to line up my shots. We talked about our days. We became friends.

And along the way, without saying one word about my misbehavior at school, Sister Elizabeth fixed the problem. At first, I started to dial back my class clownery in just her class—I didn't want to do anything to jeopardize our Thursdays. But then I'd see her looking at me through the doorway on one of my trips to the principal's office, her class erupting in applause. I didn't want to upset her. So I stopped making disruptive comments altogether. My relationships with my other teachers improved, and I was no longer Our Lady of Lourdes's class clown.

No amount of threatening, punishing, or bargaining had solved this problem—building trust in a relationship did. I worked hard to control my impulsiveness because of my personal connection with Sister Elizabeth. I was motivated to improve because of that relationship.

Was there an adult who had this kind of connection with you when you were a child? Do you remember how it impacted your motivation to do well? What are some ways you could build similar relationships with the young people you work with?

> Knowing your students is especially critical when they have a disability. It's helpful to ask parents to provide or create (some will already have one) a guidebook of sorts detailing important individualized information about their child (e.g., how they communicate: verbally, ASL, picture boards; what they crave/resist; triggers, signs that they are becoming agitated; what calms them down).

> Yes, this information can help us be an extension of their family, love the way God made them, and support their successful inclusion!

The Power of Building Relationships

Think about how it feels when an acquaintance struggles to remember your name. They stumble through an awkward "How's it going?" while frantically scrolling through a mental directory. When that happens to me, I feel very small and unimportant. Compare that to when someone smiles confidently and calls you by name without hesitation. You feel seen, cared for, visible. The point being, learn your students' names as quickly as you can, and then greet them by name every time you gather. Learn things about their lives outside the classroom. On the first day of class, invite them to fill out a Getting to Know Me survey about their favorite foods, TV shows, sports, and hobbies (you can find a sample form on page 170). Reference those surveys throughout the year, incorporating their interests into your lessons. Students will be delighted when you serve their favorite snack, mention their hobby, or play their favorite song as they enter, long after they told you in the survey!

DISCOVER AND CELEBRATE LEARNERS' GIFTS

Consider the following well-known Scripture passage:

> Now there are varieties of gifts, but the same Spirit;
>
> and there are varieties of services, but the same Lord;
>
> and there are varieties of activities, but it is the same God who activates all of them in everyone.
>
> To each is given the manifestation of the Spirit for the common good.
>
> To one is given through the Spirit utterance of wisdom, and to another the utterance of knowledge according to the same Spirit,
>
> to another faith by the same Spirit, to another gifts of healing by the one Spirit,
>
> to another the working of miracles, to another prophecy, to another the discernment of spirits,
>
> to another various kinds of tongues, to another the interpretation of tongues.
>
> All these are activated by one and the same Spirit, who allots to each one individually just as the Spirit chooses.

(1 Corinthians 12:4–11)

We all have gifts. We all have strengths. Sometimes they are hard to see because of other challenging behavior. Be the teacher or catechist who finds the spark in each of his or her learners, takes genuine delight in them, and publicly celebrates their giftedness. This is especially important for the learners in your class who have disabilities. Too often, adults focus only on their disabilities, and many completely miss the individual's strengths. And sometimes, a learner's specific strengths may not manifest in a typical linguistic-focused lesson plan. Make sure to include activities that tap into multiple intelligences—musical, kinesthetic, and spatial—to reveal students' strengths that might not otherwise be discovered. You can also rely on parents and relatives of students with disabilities to find out more about your students' strengths!

STRATEGIES TO BUILD CONNECTIONS WITH YOUR LEARNERS

The best learning takes place in the context of positive, caring relationships. Taking steps to connect with your students will dramatically impact their motivation to learn, cooperate, work hard, and contribute to the class.

Invite Students to Develop Rules

It's difficult to develop a relationship with someone when one person has all the power. As educators, we must try to share our control and sometimes let the students decide what the rules will be, what direction the class will go, and what activities they will engage in. They will then be able to choose areas of affinity and competence in the work they do.

For example, instead of deciding the class rules yourself, allow the students to develop their own rules. You can provide the categories, such as "how we participate in class" or "how we speak to one another," and facilitate a consensus on the shared values or rules. When students create their own standards, they are much more likely to follow and even defend them. Learners with neurological differences such as ADHD and autism have often inadvertently broken the rules that were imposed on them. Giving them the opportunity to offer input on these rules can help them feel more empowered.

> I often say that the more choices you give people, the more people you serve! Learners with autism in particular often live with high levels of anxiety every day. Providing them with a choice allows them to feel in control and lessens their anxiety.

> So true, and offering choices ultimately reduces the chances that the learner will become upset and exhibit the challenging behaviors that make it difficult for catechists to serve kids with disabilities.

Make Learning Fun

Many educators often rely on round-robin reading, having students take turns reading the textbook out loud. Though common, this method is often not effective. Instead, create captivating, hands-on, entertaining lessons that will contribute to a climate conducive to relationship building. For example, look for creative features in TV talk shows that you could incorporate, or use songs or hobbies that are popular with kids.

Share Personal Stories

To have close relationships with your students, they need to know that you are a human being with family, friends, and a life! Open up and share stories from your life that relate to the topic you are teaching. Did you get to know me a little better after reading my class clown story on page 124? Your personal stories will create pathways of commonality, connecting you to your students.

Create Celebration Rituals

Design and maintain a system of celebration, with opportunities for students to celebrate one another's accomplishments and contributions every time they gather. Here are some ways to celebrate on a regular basis.

- **Appreciation Bulletin Board:** Install a cork- or whiteboard in the learning space and have either sticky notes or dry erase markers available for learners to leave little comments of appreciation for one another, like "Hooray for Jorge for sharing his textbook with me when I forgot mine." The catechist can assist those with disabilities who need support in writing.

- **Verbal Celebrations:** At the end of each class, allow students the opportunity to say and hear positive comments about one another. This builds community and belonging.

- **Shared Goals and Projects:** Include service, fundraisers, and other shared projects for the group, and celebrate their progress on this shared goal regularly. For example, you could invite your students to collect and donate blankets for the homeless.

- **Laugh and Share Joy with Them:** You may have gotten some "Don't smile till Christmas" advice from educators who think the only way to keep students under control is to maintain a strict and harsh demeanor. This is nonsense. Seek out moments with them when you can laugh with abandon! Show them that your relationship with God is one centered in joy! As written in the Gospel of John, "I came that they may have life, and have it abundantly" (10:10).

Treat Them with Respect

At the core of every good relationship is a commitment to treating one another with care and kindness. Speak to students with the same tone and respect that you would another adult.

Listen to Them

As our lives fill up with more responsibilities, we attend to one another less and less. Giving a student your full attention is a tremendous gift that he or she will greatly appreciate.

Keep Appropriate Boundaries

Needless to say—and yet essential to mention—is that these practices must be implemented within appropriate boundaries. Share stories, but not overly personal ones that would be inappropriate for children.

- Keep your stories brief for those with attention differences, and make sure the words you use are well-known and understandable by those with cognitive disabilities. Avoid using idioms that a learner might interpret literally, such as, "Time to get this show on the road!"

- Give students choices but not the freedom to make choices detrimental to the class. For example, allowing a student to pick a saint to draw a picture of gives the student freedom. But allowing students to choose how many students are in their small group may result in social-coordination disaster. Learners with impulsivity challenges also may not always choose wisely.

- Build relationships, and be one *with* your students, not one *of* them.

> At times, behavioral and emotional disabilities create situations that are stressful for the catechist or teacher, making it difficult for him or her to offer the learner his or her best response. One way to stay calm and patient is to remember how stressful things are for the learner with disabilities in that moment and throughout their lives. Their behavior is not willful, nor is it about us. We are needed by them more in these moments than at any other time. We must be as generous as possible with our love and respect.

Amen!

Keep in mind that our job is to meet the learners where they are and interact in ways that match their capabilities. For example, physical affection such as pats on the back and side hugs can be an important part of developing relationships with your students, but many students with disabilities are not comfortable with hugs or handshakes. Talk to your students and their parents to find out what is appropriate for each person.

Own Your Mistakes

When you mess up, take responsibility and apologize to the students. Acknowledging that you're not perfect will make you more approachable and genuine in the eyes of your students.

Share Your Faith

No amount of instruction will come close to matching your impact as a devoted follower of Christ. Don't hide your faith under a bushel basket—let your light shine! As written in Matthew 5:14–16, "You are the light of the world. A city set on a mountain cannot be hidden. Nor do they light a lamp and then put it under a bushel basket; it is set on a lampstand, where it gives light to all in the house. Just so, your light must shine before others, that they may see your good deeds and glorify your heavenly Father."

STRATEGIES TO BUILD CONNECTIONS BETWEEN LEARNERS

While building successful relationships with your students is critical, it's just as important to facilitate relationship development and social-coordination skills among your students. Typically, learning how to make a friend, get along with others, and work in small groups are skills that adults simply expect their learners to develop. Little time is spent overtly teaching and practicing these skills. Consider the following strategies for improving social coordination in your classroom:

Community-Building Activities

Sometimes lesson plans can be too focused on information sharing. When designing or tweaking lesson plans, be sure that they include opportunities for students to share, listen, and connect with one another on an emotional level. For an example of how to do so, see the activity on the next page.

Small-Group Work

Think about a time when you were at a party with a group of adults talking. Did you behave differently when speaking with a group versus one-on-one? How does the number of people in the conversation impact how you feel and interact?

The larger the small group, the more complex and demanding the interaction becomes. Each new person who joins the group adds to the airtime, references, agreements and disagreements, etc.

Students vary in their ability to be effective in small groups, depending on the number of participants. Some can be successful in a pair but not in a group of three. Because of the increasing complexity, I recommend that no small groups be larger than four or five at the most. Some learners have difficulty even working in pairs. Having poor social-coordination skills is a common characteristic of students with autism and other neurological differences. We can help by reducing the size of small groups to match the ability of the learner and by helping him or her grow in the ability to coordinate.

Group work has its own challenges, doesn't it? To help learners who are shy or introverted get airtime in groups, try the "mutual invitation method." During a small-group activity, a group member will invite another person to share. That person can say "pass" and invite someone else to share or answer. This method helps everyone listen and feel included. For learners with more complex social-interaction challenges, identify a peer or adult mentor to assist as needed. For someone who doesn't understand that discussion time is shared, limit the number of questions or comments they can express. This helps them to prioritize their thoughts—a good skill to practice.

Great addition. Thank you! 🙏

Because of this variation in abilities, lesson plans that specify small-group numbers should be modified to allow for different groupings and to accommodate learners' varying social-coordination skill levels. Alternatively, you could impose a group number, though this often results in some learners withdrawing, disrupting, or becoming emotionally upset because they don't have the ability to coordinate with so many people at the same time.

In addition, overt social-coordination teaching and practice helps students gradually improve their referencing, listening, and communication skills to graduate to the next level, slowly increasing the number of people they can successfully coordinate with.

Successful Conversation Skills

Conversation is one of the most difficult skills in the world to master. Even some adult professionals can feel uncomfortable when they have to carry on a conversation with someone new. Learners with autism and other neurological differences often have a very difficult time conversing with others. They may get "stuck" on a topic of interest to them and not see that the topic is not so interesting to others. Providing scripting, guidance, and practice for learners with disabilities can open the door to more meaningful relationships for them. The following activity will help learners with autism and other neurological differences that impact social coordination practice these skills.

Activity: Practicing Conversation Skills

To help your learners put these tips to use, try this activity.

1. Write down on slips of paper places where conversations might take place: on an airplane, on the first day of school, at the park, at a comic book convention, etc. Place the pieces of paper in a hat.

2. Invite two to three learners to come to the front of the class and pick a conversation setting out of the hat. They will then base their conversation on that place. For students who struggle, give examples of things they could say. If a student makes an inappropriate comment, gently coach him or her by saying, "You could say that, sure. But do you think that would make the other person feel welcome?"

3. To increase the fun, add some outrageous locations to the hat, like the moon, a prehistoric jungle, or heaven. Extra points for those who guess the setting based on the conversation!

Conversation skills are essential for success. Remember, every lifelong friendship, fifty-year marriage, and successful business partnership began with that first conversation. And you don't get a second chance to make a good first impression. Unfortunately, this skill is not often overtly taught or practiced. To help your learners grow in their conversation skills, teach them to begin and maintain a conversation after being introduced. If in a triad, the person who's introducing will be responsible for making sure the conversation goes well. You could invite students to discuss their travels, favorite books or movies, or current events.

You can convey to your learners that they should make sure the conversation remains respectful, balanced, and interesting. They can ask questions and share observations and always remember that the purpose of small talk is to build relationships. Here are a few tips you can offer learners as they practice in pairs.

- Smile and keep your dialogue friendly.

- Maintain eye contact. (However, do not require this for students with autism or another disability that impacts their ability to look someone in the eye.)

- Ask appropriate questions.

- Listen carefully. (See the next section for tips on how to teach this skill.)

- Try to stay away from trite topics, like the weather, and focus on commonalities, current events, or pop culture.

- Don't use off-color humor or discuss vulgar, inappropriate topics. Explain to your students that this may offend or put off the other person and put an end to the conversation.

- Balance the airtime so that, to the degree it's possible, each party is given equal time to speak.

- Do not gossip.

- If possible, imagine that you're speaking to a sibling or cousin or pet, making the conversation feel as natural as possible.

- Help learners with autism and other disabilities improve their conversation skills by being nonjudgmental and patient and by providing a safe setting in which to practice.

- Try not to pull topics out of the air, like "So . . . what's your favorite color?"

- Try to avoid topics like politics or religion. Instead, choose other topics that connect to the setting or person you're talking to.

- Avoid complaining. Instead, ask questions about the other person, sympathize, or practice active listening.

Listening Skills

Good listening skills are essential in forming and maintaining relationships, learning, and enjoying life. We always appreciate those in our lives who take the time to listen to us, especially when we're upset. Here are a few ways to be a good listener and to practice becoming a better one that you can share with your students.

- Remain silent while the other person is talking.
- Maintain eye contact, unless a neurological difference makes this difficult. For these learners, invite them to be open about their disability, sharing, "I have autism, which makes it difficult for me to look you in the eye. Please know that I am listening even though I may be looking elsewhere."
- Be an active listener. Nod your head as the person is talking to show that you hear what he or she says.
- Ask the person to explain if you are confused.
- Ask the person questions. Students could ask about the person's family, how many siblings she has, where he grew up, what brought him to the place he's at now. Or they could ask them if they've seen a new movie or read an interesting, popular book. Or they could just ask the person to tell them about him- or herself, which could lead in many different, fascinating directions.
- Try to be respectful in your body language. Avoid slouching, crossing your arms, or facing away from the other person.
- Don't judge or criticize the person talking, and try to respect his or her feelings.
- Although tempting, try not to offer the person advice. Just being listened to is often what the person really needs. If asked, then you can offer advice.

Teaching and Modeling Acceptance

An essential factor in building social-coordination skills is acknowledging that people function differently in their approach to and interaction in relationships. Learners with disabilities often speak, move, and interact in ways that are different from typical learners. Teach and model acceptance of differences in the ways that students speak, react, and interact with one another, making it a safe, nonjudgmental environment in which to grow in their abilities to connect with others in the Body of Christ.

Activity: Practicing Listening Skills

1. Pair up students and invite each learner to tell a story that addresses one of the following criteria: a time they were frustrated, a time they had fun, or a time they tried something new.

2. After each learner has had an opportunity to share, have the pair reflect on their own listening skills during the activity. Were you able to maintain eye contact? Can you remember the details that were shared? Did you ask relevant questions?

You may not have class time to devote to exclusively practicing conversation, listening, and other skills, but you can still integrate chances to practice into your lesson plan. For example, invite students to discuss the topic of your catechetical lesson in a conversation. If you are teaching about the Beatitudes, your conversation-practice topics might include the following:

- What does it mean to be "poor in spirit"?
- Why is it important to be a peacemaker?
- Talk with a friend about a time when you felt persecuted for your faith.

Doing so helps to maintain the integrity of the lesson while helping learners improve their listening and conversation skills—lifelong and necessary abilities.

Three Takeaways

- Identifying the gifts of your learners helps build connections and confidence—particularly for learners with disabilities.

- Just as important as building relationships with your students is building relationships between them. Creating opportunities to better learners' conversation and listening skills is a lesson that will serve them for life.

- Learners with disabilities often speak, move, and interact in ways that are different from typical learners. Teach and model acceptance of the differences in the ways that learners interact with one another.

LOOKING AHEAD...

- What are the strengths and gifts of the learners with disabilities that you work with?

- How do you/will you recognize and celebrate those strengths?

- What system of celebration could you add to your teaching to provide opportunities to celebrate one another on a regular basis?

✳ NOTES:

_____

_____

_____

_____

_____

_____

CHAPTER 12

The Ghosts of Pedagogy Past: Forming Your Teaching Style

BY JOHN E. BARONE

Getting Started

Think back to the teachers you had when you were a learner. Were they strict or lenient? Kind or mean? Rigid or flexible? Often our discipline style as catechists and teachers is a reflection of how we were treated as kids. Sometimes we emulate the great teachers in our past. Sometimes we try not to follow the example of those not-so-great teachers in our past. And sometimes we've been handed techniques that may not be the best for learning outcomes, particularly for those with disabilities. In this chapter, I hope to help you find a balanced disciplinary style, with just the right combination of loving care and firm boundaries and consequences that will work for all learners. And who knows, maybe a few of your learners will emulate your style further down the line.

TWO-MINUTE CHECK-IN

- How would you describe your teaching style?

- Did you learn this style from a particular teacher or administrator?

- How successful and effective do you believe your teaching style is?

The Adaptive Teacher ➡ Faith-Based Strategies to Reach and Teach Learners with Disabilities

THE TOUGH "OLD-SCHOOL" TEACHING MODEL

I look back fondly and perhaps a bit fearfully on my early years in Catholic elementary school under the regime of the principal, Sister John the Baptist. She and the other sisters were tough. Strict. We had to sit up straight, eyes up front, feet on the floor. We moved around school grounds in single file, with our gaze fixed on the back of the head in front of us. If we got out of line . . . *whack!* After all these years, the memory of the sting of the yardstick across my knuckles still hasn't faded.

The sisters' expectations were clearly communicated and consistently enforced. If we broke a rule, we were punished, often in unpleasant ways. I remember when Sister Catherine Margaret caught me chewing gum in second grade. She made me drop it on the floor and push it all the way to the trash can with my nose. Sister was trying to manage my behavior by using humiliation, which is not only hurtful to the child but also not very effective in changing behaviors. I still chewed gum after that; I was just sneakier about it.

From first through fifth grade, constant discipline was my world. And with adolescence approaching, I was in for a wild ride. But then one day, without notice, those sisters moved out of the convent, and the "Kumbaya" sisters moved in. Their first teaching: Jesus loves me!

> **Humiliating learners in the classroom is right up there with using sarcasm. For learners, there is nothing comical about being on the receiving end of biting remarks. No pun intended, but the word "sarcasm" comes from the Greek verb *sarkazein,* which initially meant "to tear flesh like a dog"!**

> *An apt word, I think. Humor at someone else's expense is never funny, i.m.o.* 😞

THE WARM "NEW SCHOOL" TEACHING MODEL

The "Kumbaya" sisters, as we'll call them, were warm and caring. Everything was love and dove and peace and joy. We got to experience hugs for the first time at school. They played guitar and sang. They got to know us. They *smiled* at us.

Cruel and meaningless punishments ended and were replaced by meaningful consequences that taught us the reasons for the rules. Remember my gum-pushing episode with Sister Catherine Margaret? However unpleasant, I still chewed gum. One day after the "Kumbaya" sisters moved in, I was caught chewing gum by Sister Pat. Sister asked me to spit out the gum and to join her after school to talk about the incident. The "Oooh!" and "You're in trouble!" comments from fellow classmates notwithstanding, I was genuinely curious about how Sister Pat would handle the situation.

When I arrived, Sister Pat asked me, "Do you know why we have a rule against chewing gum?" She didn't appear angry. I didn't understand. Why wasn't she yelling? Why was she smiling?

"Um, I don't know, Sister."

Sister Pat grinned, and with a whooshing sound that would have made Bruce Lee proud, she whipped out a paint scraper and cheerfully announced, "Well, you're about to find out!" She handed me the scraper and gave me instructions to spend the next hour scraping gum from underneath the desktops in the classroom. At the end of that disgusting hour, it was crystal clear why we had a rule against chewing gum. (Although I must concede that I found the myriad stages of gum decay to be fascinating.)

From that day forward, I never chewed gum again at school. Sister Catherine Margaret's "Nose Olympics" punishment was not only humiliating, it was ineffective. It didn't *teach* me anything. Sister Pat's intervention incorporated the principle of rationality: she chose a consequence that would help me understand the reason for the rule. And in so doing, she enlisted me in the ranks of those who would subsequently follow and ultimately *defend* the classroom standard of avoiding gum. From that day on, when I saw schoolmates chewing gum, I would flash back to that interminable hour of scraping and find myself telling others to "spit it out!"

TOP-TEN LIST OF "OLD-SCHOOL" INTERVENTION BENEFITS

Delivering meaningful consequences was one of many techniques I took from the "Kumbaya" sisters' playbook, but there were benefits that came with Sister John the Baptist's intervention style as well. Even though some of their techniques didn't take into consideration the needs of learners with disabilities, their practices still hold many benefits for them. Those who were taught by Sister John the Baptist's staff will tell you that, though they were sometimes tough, the sisters still had a positive impact on their learners. Here's why.

10. **Students were held accountable for their actions.** Even though we didn't always do the right thing, it was clear that when we didn't, the school (and our parents) would hold us accountable. This expectation helped us become adults who take responsibility for our choices.

9. **Students weren't rescued from suffering the natural consequences of their bad choices.** If there was discomfort associated with the consequences of our actions, we weren't rescued or excused. The pain we experienced motivated us to do better the next time. We grew up to be adults who see failure as an opportunity to grow.

8. **Students were less entitled.** It was *impossible* to be a spoiled, entitled child in this environment, and we grew up believing that the world didn't owe us anything. We became more resourceful and industrious.

7. **Students became adept at problem solving.** The sisters wouldn't remove obstacles for us. They challenged us to figure out how to go around or over or through them. Doing so gave us lots of practice in problem solving and helped us become high-achieving adults.

6. **Students learned to make amends for their actions when they resulted in damage to the community.** When I wrote "John loves Laurie" in permanent ink on the top of a lunchroom table in eighth grade, I spent an entire Saturday scrubbing it off. There were many occasions when I had to "pay back" for my actions that negatively impacted the community. This approach gave us the ability to see beyond our own needs when making decisions and choices and to consider the needs of the community as well.

5. **Students' achievement matched and often exceeded their potential.** Sister John the Baptist and friends set the bar high for everybody, which made us want to do our very best to live up to it. Their high expectations helped create adults who have big dreams and the confidence to achieve them.

4. **Students became resilient.** Simply put, we were knocked down a lot by the sisters. We learned to get up, dust ourselves off, and try again. We grew up to be adults who keep going when the going gets tough.

3. **Students weren't coddled.** Mick Jagger was sharing the same message as Sister John the Baptist at that time: "You Can't Always Get What You Want." We weren't indulged. As a result, we grew up to be adults with realistic expectations.

2. **Students learned to adapt to the system.** While we will address the importance of the system accommodating the learner later in the chapter, there is value in the learners' ability to develop flexibility in response to expectations that are not so flexible. This experience led to adults who are able to succeed even in less than ideal environments (i.e., in interactions with difficult people, bosses, coworkers, etc.).

1. **Students learned a lot about their Catholic faith.** Although the sisters were strict, they were passionate about forming their learners in the faith, and this commitment resulted in many adults who are devoted to Christ and the Church. Even though they could be a bit draconian in their methods, Sister John the Baptist and friends contributed a great deal to my growth in knowledge, skill, and character. For these contributions, I remain eternally grateful.

TOP-TEN LIST OF "NEW SCHOOL" INTERVENTION BENEFITS

When the "Kumbaya" sisters moved in, they brought a very different approach to pedagogy and behavior management, resulting in positive contributions as well as some not-so-helpful attitudes and practices. Let's begin with the positive.

10. **Students were invited into relationship with the faculty.** We feared the strict sisters, and we respected them, but we didn't really know them. With the "Kumbaya" sisters, my peers and I were allowed and encouraged to develop close relationships with our teachers. Knowing them led to trusting them, which led to loving them.

9. **Students' relationships with one another were encouraged and nurtured.** Relationships existed among us students before, but they weren't fostered until the "Kumbaya" sisters arrived. The sisters integrated community- and relationship-building activities into the curriculum, resulting in meaningful friendships among the students. Their emphasis on social-coordination skills led to our ability to maintain healthy relationships.

8. **Students were challenged to think critically.** Before, when asked for our opinion in class, we weren't really able to answer. We were used to being told what to think. The "Kumbaya" sisters taught us *how* to think. They directed our questions back to us. And instead of just memorizing facts about our faith, we were challenged to apply what the Church and our parents taught us and decide what was right or wrong. Their emphasis on critical thinking led to our ability to discern and make sound moral judgments.

7. **Students were challenged to think creatively.** With the previous sisters, order was more important than creativity. Coloring outside the lines was discouraged. With the new sisters, we were encouraged to think outside the box, to reject the typical, and to dig deep for the unusual. This gift stayed with us, and we continue to apply innovation and ingenuity in our work and in our play.

6. **Students felt safe in the "Kumbaya" climate.** More than ever before, we felt safe to take risks, to try new things, and to trust one another with our vulnerabilities. We weren't afraid to be wrong, to make a mistake, or to fail. We enjoy the fruits of this climate as adults who are more confident and willing to take chances.

5. **Students were allowed choices in the curriculum.** The "Kumbaya" sisters understood that providing choices would give learners the ability to choose directions that matched their competencies and affinities, resulting in a higher motivation to participate and achieve. This "do what you love" emphasis stayed with us as fellow classmates and I chose vocational paths of fulfillment and contribution.

4. **Student infractions were framed as learning opportunities rather than as moral failures.** Whenever we missed the mark, these sisters would see the behavior as a chance to teach rather than scold. They maintained the role of ally—not opponent—and we learned to rely on them rather than resist. Those of us who chose teaching as a career paid it forward and offered this same support to the children in our care.

3. **Students experienced more joy and laughter.** Laughter, which once was seen as the enemy of authority, was now welcome in the classroom. Learning became delightful. Many of us now carry with us the view that learning is a lifelong, joyful pursuit.

2. **Students were free to express their thoughts and feelings.** Because of terrifying cold calls and shaming when we got an answer wrong, we were a bit hesitant to share our thoughts or feelings with the strict sisters. The "Kumbaya" sisters encouraged us to say what we thought and to share how we felt. We learned to respectfully share and to honor those whose thoughts and feelings were different from ours. Although middle-school students are not always accepting of their peers, the "Kumbaya" sisters' acceptance of us led to our accepting one another.

1. **Students' faith formation was centered in a relationship with Christ.** The sisters led us toward a close personal friendship with Jesus, expanding our belief from our heads to our hearts and investing in our future faith. We were transformed by their work.

TOWARD A COMBINED APPROACH

Clearly, the work of the "Kumbaya" sisters was phenomenal, but like the strict sisters, they had their weaknesses as well. They tended to be too lenient, allowing learners to slide when they needed to be held accountable. Their classroom management was often too loose, and without fixed procedures and boundaries, classrooms would sometimes get out of control. These sisters would also often carry learners through a difficulty rather than challenge them to go outside their comfort zone and struggle for success.

Some teachers or catechists make the mistake of following the "Kumbaya" sisters' lead by coddling learners with disabilities. However, the weaknesses in this approach prompt caretakers to be too lenient. We need to remember that it is *more* important for students with disabilities to develop independence and ownership, not less. They should not be "carried" by adults but encouraged to become as self-sufficient as possible.

I feel blessed to have experienced both of these styles growing up. Their teaching has informed my philosophy of education. From the "Kumbaya" sisters' playbook, I took that good education takes place in the context of loving, caring relationships, and from the strict sisters' playbook, that children do best when they take ownership of their lives and are allowed to suffer the natural consequences of their actions.

Combining their approaches creates loving, relationship-centered learning that allows students to work toward full ownership of their academic and social development, leading to young adults who are competent, confident, and able to function independently.

Concrete Strategies to Foster Ownership in Young People

Here are a few ways to help young people take such ownership of their work—particularly learners with disabilities.

HELP LEARNERS TAKE OWNERSHIP OF THEIR BELONGINGS

A first-year teacher in my summer program once came to me with a backpack a student had left behind on the playground. "Where is the Lost and Found?" she asked.

I said, "We don't have a Lost and Found. We believe that having a Lost and Found steals the opportunity for learners with poor materials-management skills to suffer the natural consequences of leaving their stuff lying around. Please put it back where you found it."

She was horrified. It sounds mean, doesn't it? But it's the loving thing to do. Imagine you had a personal assistant who would pick up and return any items you left behind throughout your day. Would you be motivated to get better at keeping track of your belongings? I wouldn't! While adults may feel that these actions are kind and caring, this behavior actually creates a dependency on them and a low motivation for learners to grow in these management skills.

So, when you see student belongings left on your campus, let them lie. When learners must track their belongings back to where they left them, or if their items are lost or damaged, they will feel more motivated to improve in their ability to manage their belongings.

Application for Learners with Disabilities

Learners with ADHD and other disabilities often have poor materials-management skills. They frequently misplace or forget items that they need. One strategy that can be helpful is a materials-management checklist posted where it will be seen often (like on the fridge) to use in the evening in preparation for the next day. The learner references the schedule and checks off each item as he or she packs it. This strategy can help learners depend less on others to take care of their belongings. On page 147 is an example of a materials-management checklist.

PROMPT LEARNERS INSTEAD OF REMINDING THEM

Another teaching behavior that can create dependency is our tendency to remind learners—that they left a water bottle behind or to turn in their homework the next day. Which, again, feels like a loving thing. In our doing so, however, learners become dependent on adults to steer them through their day, and without that support, they aren't able to keep up with their responsibilities.

The extreme method is to say nothing at all and allow the learner to forget and miss out. If you're too softhearted for this method, try prompting instead. Ask rather than tell. The learner will then figure out what he or she needs to do.

Here are a few examples of the difference between prompting and reminding.

Reminder	Prompt
"Don't forget your backpack!"	"What are you forgetting?"
"I'll pick you up in front of the church at 11."	"When and where will I be picking you up?"
"Remember to bring your permission slip next week."	"What will you need to bring with you next week?"

With a reminder, the adult does the thinking for the learner and fosters a dependency.

With a prompt, the learner does the work, and this thinking ultimately leads him or her to ask, "Am I forgetting anything?" "What will I need to bring?" "When and where is my appointment?" without the help of an adult.

Invite Learners to Figure It out Themselves

Independence and ownership are fostered when adults don't readily provide answers or assistance but assure learners that they can solve the problem on their own.

For example, which response is more effective?

Question	Response
YOUTH: "Mom, where is my blue sweater?"	**MOM 1:** "In the third drawer of your dresser."
	MOM 2: "I'm sure you'll be able to find it."
YOUTH: "When is our Confirmation retreat?"	**CATECHIST 1:** "On Friday, January 14."
	CATECHIST 2: "Where could you find that information?"

Application for Learners with Disabilities

This self-talk is often absent in learners with disabilities. But with prompts and much practice, they will eventually ask themselves these questions without any help from an adult, leading to more autonomy and independence. For example, you can provide index cards that have self-talk questions written on them for different contexts. Parents and teachers can model self-talk for the learner by saying, "What do I need to do before leaving the classroom? Oh, I need to gather my belongings, turn out the light, etc."

Students who leave an environment where adults constantly provided reminders are typically unable to function successfully on their own. Those who were prompted have grown in their ability to take ownership and are much more successful when living independently.

Materials Checklist	Mon	Tues	Wed	Thurs	Fri	Sat	Sun
Keys	✔						
Wallet	✔						
Phone	✔						
Retainer	✔						
Notebooks and folders	✔						
Pens	✔						
Street shoes by bed	✔						
Track tests & quizzes	✔						
Gym clothes and shoes	✔						
Take pill	✔						
Lunchbox	✔						

Of course, the use of visuals would be included among prompts that are great for some learners, especially someone who doesn't speak verbally. Visuals are particularly helpful because they don't disappear as words do; they can go with the person—and they're without facial expressions!

Good addition. For learners who are nonverbal, I like to use laminated pictograms on Velcro, with a procedure to move the card from the "scheduled" side to the "finished" side of the board after completing each task depicted.

DON'T RESCUE STUDENTS

Young people who are dependent become quite adept at getting the adults in their lives to rescue them when they're in trouble. And for adults who see a learner in need, it can be all too tempting for them to jump in and fix their problems for them.

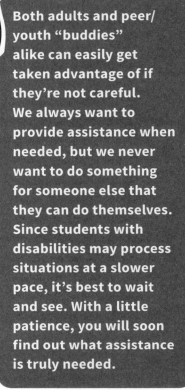

If a student starts to cry or explains his or her problem, be sure to respond with empathy rather than dismiss. A response of "too bad" or "tough luck" can be discouraging. But a caring "That must be very upsetting to you" will result in the student's feeling heard and understood. The next step is to coach the student in solving the problem with a prompt, such as "What are you going to do?" Steer him or her away from solutions that involve your fixing it.

In deciding how best to respond, consider the following conversation:

STUDENT (ON PHONE): "Dad, I left my homework on the dresser, and if I don't turn it in today, I'm going to get an F in the class!"

FATHER: "Don't worry, Son, I'll drop it off for you at lunch. Just meet me in the parking lot."

Or

STUDENT: "Dad, I left my homework on the dresser, and if I don't turn it in today, I'm going to get an F in the class!"

FATHER: "Oh, that's a shame, Son. You must be really upset. What are you going to do?"

STUDENT: (after a pause) "Well, can you get it and bring it up?"

FATHER: "No, because that's your responsibility. Let's talk tonight about a plan that will help you get better at remembering to bring your homework."

Both adults and peer/youth "buddies" alike can easily get taken advantage of if they're not careful. We always want to provide assistance when needed, but we never want to do something for someone else that they can do themselves. Since students with disabilities may process situations at a slower pace, it's best to wait and see. With a little patience, you will soon find out what assistance is truly needed.

Yes, that wait time is critical. Our desire to help others can be our greatest strength, but if we are carrying and enabling learners, we do them a disservice. The loving thing is often to let them struggle to achieve the goal on their own.

Many adults feel as though they *must* rescue when the consequences of not doing so are serious. But the longer adults wait to stop rescuing, the higher the price for the student. An F in middle school is not as serious as an F in high school, which is not as serious as an F in college. With consistent parental carrying and rescuing, the learner will not develop his problem-solving skills, and that first year away from home is not the time to start functioning independently!

However, when adults refuse to rescue learners, they build up their self-reliance and confidence.

Application for Learners with Disabilities

Sometimes, learners with disabilities can become so dependent on adults that they may use their disability to get adults to do things for them. Of course, this is not true for all learners with disabilities. By offering visual checklists (like the one on the page 147) and schedules, you can help students with disabilities check that they have everything they need, building in structure and self-reliance.

FINDING YOUR BALANCE

What kind of catechist are you? Do you lean more toward Sister John the Baptist or the "Kumbaya" sisters? In our reflection and self-evaluation, we can assess our progress. Going forward, it's important that we try to keep a balance of both styles with our learners. By combining the loving care of the "Kumbaya" sisters with the independence building of Sister John the Baptist and friends, the children in your care will grow in their ownership to the point where the role of the adults in their lives is reduced to celebrating the learners' success!

Three Takeaways

- Often, the teachers who left the greatest mark on us are the teachers we seek to emulate. In reflecting on your teaching style, assess which methods you can employ that are the most effective for your learners.

- To help learners take ownership of their lives and learning, try not to rescue them but to prompt them to take action on their own.

- Our goal as educators is to arm our learners with as much independence and ownership as possible.

LOOKING AHEAD...

◆ How have the teachers in your past influenced the kind of catechist you are?

◆ What are some things your teachers did that you emulate?

◆ What are some things your teachers did that you didn't like and thus never do?

◆ What are a few of the not-so-great teaching habits that you'd like to replace with better techniques?

❋ NOTES:

_____

_____

_____

_____

_____

_____

CHAPTER 13

Viewing Disabilities as Differences

BY CHARLEEN KATRA

Getting Started

When we speak about persons with disabilities, we may hear the phrase "We are more alike than different." This is true in many ways. Our humanity, through its divine creation, connects us together. We all have strengths, and we all have weaknesses or disabilities. In the classroom and beyond, these differences are a gift to us and to those around us—as is our ability to grow and learn. The degree to which we acknowledge and appreciate our own giftedness and limitations is the degree to which we will respond to the realities of others—a fact that becomes more evident as we age and become more dependent on others.

TWO-MINUTE CHECK-IN

- How have you been an advocate for inclusion in your parish or school?

- Have you seen a change over the years in how learners with disabilities are viewed?

- What might you do to further embrace their differences and promote inclusion in the Church and beyond?

As the Committee for the Jubilee Day of the Community with Persons with Disabilities wrote in their May 2000 paper, "Persons with disabilities are prophets of how each of us may become in the future, when physical strength diminishes, when we may lose our autonomy, become totally dependent: even then we will want to be treated with dignity and respect and still be responsible for our life and take part in community events."

As educators, we must seek ways to embrace disabilities and differences and increase access and inclusion for all people in the Church and in the world. To do this, we must first learn to see the whole person God places in front of us.

AVOIDING JUDGMENT

Have you ever read a book or watched a movie that you initially had low expectations for but then found yourself pleasantly surprised at how much you enjoyed it? Maybe the book stirred up unexpected emotions or inspired you to consider a different perspective. Maybe its impact on you turned out to be more significant than you expected. The same is true in the way we may sometimes view learners with disabilities in the classroom. For, if a book or movie can affect us so intensely, think how powerful our involvement with such learners can be when we commit to not judging them by outward appearances, stereotypes, stigmas, or others' opinions. God places every learner in front of us with complete intentionality. Our response to each learner is our response to God.

How to Better Understand the Learners We Serve

The most dedicated bishop, priest, catechist, or educator will never be an expert regarding all disabilities. And yet, we are called to learn how to better serve persons with disabilities. As the USCCB writes, "The bishops of the United States feel a concern for persons with disabilities that goes beyond their spiritual welfare to encompass their total well-being. This concern should find expression at all levels."

PARTNER WITH PARENTS

For one thing, we can tap into the wisdom of parents, who will become experts on their child's disability. They can help us understand their child and tell us his or her learning preferences as well as helpful strategies. We may find our empathy increasing the more we learn, for the child and his or her parent may live in a world of never-ending appointments with doctors and therapists. Also, most families do not plan to have a child with a disability—at birth or later in life. They, too, are navigating new and changing realities. As the U.S. Bishops' statement "Welcome and Justice for Persons with Disabilities: A Framework of Access and Inclusion" describes, many families aren't prepared for a child born with a disability or developmental differences. They write, "Our pastoral response is to become informed about disabilities and to offer ongoing support to the family and welcome to the child" (No. 9). The pressures of having a child with a disability weigh heavily on all aspects of family life—physically, emotionally, financially, and spiritually. It can weigh on the extended family as well, who may be involved in helping the family with daily activities if they live nearby.

Another issue to consider is that husbands and wives may be divided on many issues, including whether to disclose a diagnosis. Catechists and teachers often ask the question, "Why don't the parents tell us?" It's important for us to realize that one parent may want to disclose information, while the spouse may not. We must be sensitive to the fact that such issues can cause great tension at home: parents may feel guilty over the unbalanced amounts of attention offered to their children. And hence, the average divorce rate in the disability community is typically higher than in the general population.

If any population of people needs, the Church, it's this one. These families need us to open our doors and our hearts to embrace them and give them much-needed respite. We all come to Church seeking help and hope. God willing, upon arrival, they will find a Church family delighted to see them and desiring for them to stay. Everything we do for them strengthens their faith and affirms their family's Catholic identity.

EXPAND YOUR KNOWLEDGE

We can also try to deepen our knowledge about disabilities in general. For when we do so, we "put on the eyes of Christ" and see the whole person and the whole family. As educators, our goal is to affirm the humanity that every parent already sees in his or her own child.

By embracing the reality that every learner is different, we embrace the neurodiversity of all humans. And in doing so, catechists, educators, and parents pave the way for more individuals to live and learn together. Every effort that we make to understand and reach all learners makes our world a better place. Our Catholic faith calls us to the mission of accompanying others on a journey. Sometimes the journey is long, and sometimes the journey is difficult. But we are never alone. God has promised to be with us always.

As you move forward in your vocation, continue to seek out strategies and resources that support inclusion. Here are a few practical options to consider.

- **Tap professionals for more advice and invite presentations.** Be intentional in seeking out parents, teachers, catechists, and health-care professionals who can be sounding boards and offer pertinent information on an individual's diagnosis or other related topics. Invite these individuals to present on the topic of their expertise at your parish or school. Remember that parents are experts on their loved one's diagnosis. While not everyone is comfortable with public speaking, many would be delighted to do so. As an added bonus, you'll likely find individuals who can present in more than one language!

> The diagnosis is helpful in giving us a starting point, but within each diagnosis, we want to remember that there are huge variations in functioning and strengths and weaknesses. That's why it's important to reach out to others who are familiar with the individual's diagnosis.

- **Reach out to other educators.** If you are a catechist or religious educator with a learner who attends a public school, ask the parent(s)/guardian(s) for written authorization to contact the school to speak with their child's teacher(s). Public schools offer an abundance of resources for serving diverse learners. From special-education teachers to life-skills and resource-room teachers, there is a wealth of highly trained educators who are available to tap for advice. They are serving the same individual you are five days a week. Though they may be surprised to hear from you initially, most will be willing to offer best practices and the tips and tools they utilize. They want the best for this child too.

> Right. We all have a wide range of variations present in us!

Some Catholic schools have similar trained educators on staff. When we implement the same strategies at school, church, and home, the likelihood for the learner to progress academically, socially, and emotionally increases exponentially.

- **Check out Catholic resources.** Seek information from national Catholic organizations' websites, including the National Catholic Partnership on Disability, the National Catholic Education Association-Exceptional Learners Resources, the National Catholic Office for the Deaf, and others. More resources can be found on page 180.

- **Make use of diocesan resources.** Most dioceses have ministries that support outreach to individuals with disabilities as well as inclusion efforts. Connect with (arch)diocesan offices via websites, calls, and visits. You can also seek out the person responsible for supporting the inclusion of diverse learners in parishes and schools in your local church. More archdiocesan-related resources can be found on page 180.

RESOURCES FOR FAMILIES

Websites:

- Center for Parent Information and Resources' national parent centers, https://www.parentcenterhub.org/find-your-center/
- Family to Family Network, https://www.familytofamilynetwork.org
- Pathways, https://pathways.org/
- "Marriage and a Special Needs Child" article, http://www.foryourmarriage.org/marriage-and-a-special-needs-child/
- Religious Signs for Families app by the Archdiocese of Philadelphia, www.religiousaslapp.org/
- The Arc's resources for parents, https://www.thearc.org/i-am/a-parent
- Understood for Learning and Attention Issues, https://www.understood.org/en

Retreats:

- 3-Minute Retreat, https://www.loyolapress.com/our-catholic-faith/prayer/3-minute-retreats

Note: Please see page 180 for more resources for families of children with disabilities.

- **Study up on local parish offerings.** Often, parishes offer a plethora of resources for individuals with disabilities, for their families, and for inclusion opportunities and best practices for fellow parishioners. Review their websites and bulletins, make calls or visits, and have conversations with leadership and parishioners to help support your inclusion and education efforts.

- **Study up on state offerings.** Research national, state, and community organizations for secular disability-related information. Some offer free or low-cost training and resources available to all who are interested.

- **Use all resources wisely.** Take comfort in the words of Margaret Mead, an American cultural anthropologist, who said, "Never doubt that a small group of thoughtful, committed citizens can change the world; indeed, it's the only thing that ever has."

Increased awareness and access to information affords us greater opportunities to advance the inclusion of individuals with disabilities at a faster pace than ever before. Keep in mind that academic research and studies are valuable, but the ability to gain practical, successful strategies, and implement them with pastoral care, is invaluable!

ASSESS PHYSICAL SPACES

If your parish property was built or renovated in recent decades, it likely includes features designed to improve accessibility. In architecture, this practice is known as Universal Design: design plans that intentionally aim to create environments usable by everyone. When access for persons with disabilities is incorporated into building designs from the start, it removes additional labor and costs to correct for various needs later. Though structures such as ramps were primarily intended for persons using wheelchairs, the elderly who use walkers and young families who push strollers and even the parish staff who frequently need to move equipment and materials on carts between buildings also benefit from them.

In recent years, this concept has been embraced in learning environments as well. Similar to making physical structures more accommodating for all, Universal Design for Learning (UDL) is a framework that takes into account the needs of all learners. One key way that this is accomplished is by addressing the issue of educational barriers from the outset. Ensuring that barriers do not exist to inhibit one's access to learning makes the need to invest time and finances later to remove barriers unnecessary. Combined proactive approaches such as these level the playing field, or learning environment. Remember the phrase "Give a person a fish, you feed him or her for a day; teach a person to fish, you feed him or her for life"? It sounds like great advice until we think in terms of UDL. Before any fishing or learning can occur, an individual must first be able to obtain access to the shoreline. That means eliminating "one size fits all" thinking and providing varied and flexible goals, methods, and materials and appropriate supports and accommodations for learners. When we adjust and customize our space and teaching to meet each individual's needs, we make learning accessible, fun, and engaging for all.

KEY TAKEAWAYS FOR SERVING LEARNERS WITH DISABILITIES

Shame and guilt played a prevalent role in disability history. Fortunately, more and more educators, parents, and medical experts are embracing differences as opportunities to learn and practice new and creative responses. The fact that diverse learners, by their very nature, inspire and encourage educators and parents to do things differently—in other words, more creatively—is reason enough to celebrate the gifts they offer for the greater good.

Here are a few important reminders and strategies to consider to better serve all learners.

- **See and teach the learner, not the disability or difference.** Individuals with disabilities have relationships and interests—they are social beings. Don't allow a diagnosis or a disability label to place limits on them. As much as you can, see their whole selves and their potential.

- **Be an advocate for inclusion.** As much as possible, seek out opportunities for groups of diverse learners to learn and be together. Help others embrace a culture of differences, not disabilities. Too often, as learners with a diagnosis grow older, their social opportunities diminish. The more we promote full inclusion at all ages and stages, the better their lives will be. It's also important to teach others about inclusion strategies and share your information and passion—they can be contagious. Be a living witness to gospel values of social justice and inclusion.

- **Appreciating differences means doing some things differently.** Being aware of your learners' age and ability differences and taking those into account in your activities and resources can help respect the dignity of your learners and make learning more accessible. It's also important to be sensitive to an individual's cognitive ability. Materials and language used can inadvertently limit expectations. Modify and adapt your resources according to the real needs of the learner during all stages of his or her life.

- **Model respect for all learners.** The leader sets the tone. As the leader, you set the tone for your learners. They are watching and often mimicking your every move. You have a privilege and a responsibility to convey a clear message about the distinct value of every learner present.

- **Use resources generally used by other learners.** Sometimes a varied or unique plan or resource is not necessary. Whenever possible, utilize the same means that you would for other learners (e.g., technology). Inquire directly with the learner about specific needs or supports if he or she is able to self-advocate. This promotes self-determination and self-advocacy skills.

NURTURING THE GIFTS OF ALL LEARNERS

The United States Conference of Catholic Bishops writes, "All persons with disabilities have the capacity to proclaim the Gospel and to be living witnesses to its truth within the community of faith and offer valuable gifts. Their involvement enriches every aspect of Church life. They are not just the recipients of catechesis—they are also its agents" (No. 49). When we reflect on Scripture, we are reminded that every time Jesus is present, the story has both a social and a spiritual dimension. He is commonly among the very people others thought were unworthy of his attention. Jesus always saw their gifts rather than their differences. Jesus embraced the diversity created by his Father to offer the lessons our world continues to need.

The more we can begin to shift from using the term *disabilities* to the term *differences*, the more we open up a world of positive implications. And the more our actions and words shift from exclusion to inclusion, judgment to appreciation, the more we embrace the normalcy of differences apparent in disabilities.

MOVING FORWARD

When we view disabilities as differences—as diversity—we will better include diverse learners and add to the dignity and integrity of the learning environment. The presence of diverse learners brings about change, energy, and openness. When neurological differences are respected and valued with the same passion and integrity we afford other variations in humanity, such as race, ethnicity, and religion, our world will be one step closer to becoming a more just society. As educators, we strive to develop the full potential of every learner by maximizing his or her natural God-given strengths. Ultimately, when we let go of our desire to change learners into people they are not and embrace them for who they are, we will have arrived at the intersection of love and harmony initially intended by God.

Three Takeaways

- The more we see beyond the disability to the whole person, the better we serve our learners, model respect, and carry out God's mission.

- Partnering with parents, understanding terminology, and assessing our physical spaces are just a few of the ways we can deepen our understanding of learners with disabilities.

- Shifting from using the term *disabilities* to using *differences* will help us better move from exclusion to inclusion and model respect in the world.

 LOOKING AHEAD...

◆ Which disabilities did you learn something new about?

◆ What are you willing to do differently now to teach diverse learners?

◆ How will you be an advocate for inclusion in your parish? Family? Community?

✳ NOTES:

Conclusion

The book is finished!

Yes, so exciting!

I wanted to thank you for sharing in the writing of this book. You have been such a joy to work with, and what you've shared with the readers will be so helpful.

It's been a great experience, and I'm glad to have done so with you, John! I always knew that we shared a passion for inclusion, and this book makes that clear.

I'm glad you started chapter 1 by emphasizing the importance of a warm welcome for all learners and the special importance to those with disabilities. Throughout my schooling, I've had teachers and catechists who ignored us, rushed around to get things ready, or worse, made us line up in single file in silence when we entered the classroom. I like your way better!

That seemingly simple "ministry of presence" can be very comforting to someone with high anxiety. I enjoyed your comical but truth-bearing analogies, especially the one about whether someone chooses to daydream (bologna sandwich in church) or not. 😄 How we frame inattention, viewing it in terms of the person's character or development, makes a big difference in how we respond.

Thanks. That daydream actually happened! And no, it wasn't willful. Your explanation of all the executive functions in chapter 5 will be a great tool for catechists to use when they encounter unexpected behaviors from diverse learners. Being able to view those behaviors through a developmental frame rather than as a function of character is one of the top-five most important points in our book. Old-school scolding has got to go!

There's certainly info in this book that we would all do well to take our time reflecting on, like the dignity of the person and the urgent need for social justice in a world that's more diverse than ever. But your chapter "Courtesy Can Be Kryptonite" offers a beautifully straightforward approach to regaining command of a situation by simply saying "You may" instead of begging "Please!" I hope catechists, teachers, and parents run with that quick, effective tip!!

Yeah, I'm amazed at how much more compliant kids become when that phrasing is used. And they're less entitled. Language is powerful! The People-First Language you discuss in chapter 1 is another example of that. It's so important not to define people by their disabilities or use outdated, hurtful words like *handicapped* or *retarded*. 😔

Growth is a process, but it does take some intentionality, too. If this book helps readers increase their ability to see and celebrate the giftedness of every learner, then it will have opened the doors of the Church to more families. For, those families have a Catholic identity that needs to be supported, nourished, and affirmed.

Yes, and I think our readers will be more open to providing that support, nourishment, and affirmation in surprising and new ways, like using fidget objects and other sensory-integration tools, as well as the accommodations and modifications we've shared.

Right—there is a learning curve. But, anything worthwhile . . . 😊 Bottom line, my friend, is that people who have greater needs need others more. Getting to know learners (it's always about relationships!) and finding out what supports are needed, such as using a mini trampoline or extending the time allowed to do an activity, will help make their participation more meaningful. To me, the litmus test is when it's a joyful experience for everyone involved. That's our goal!

Well, writing this book with you has certainly accomplished that goal. You've brought me much joy! Okay, ready to start the sequel?! But seriously, this has been so fun, my friend. What a blessing you are to me and to all you touch with your ministry. 😇

🎉 🎈 I've loved working with you on this too, John! Your gifts are many. Thanks for always sharing them so generously.

 My pleasure, and I hope our readers enjoy reading this book as much as we did writing it! God is good! 🙏

 All the time!

Common Diagnoses Glossary

Anxiety disorders—A group of disorders, including Obsessive-Compulsive Disorder (OCD) and Panic Disorder, in which anxiety is difficult to manage. OCD includes unwanted and repeated thoughts, feelings, ideas, sensations, or behaviors (obsessions) that make one feel driven to do something (compulsions).

Attention deficit hyperactivity disorders (ADHD)—A group of disorders that includes three subtypes: Predominantly Hyperactive/Impulsive, Predominantly Inattentive, and Combined Types. Symptoms include difficulty staying focused and paying attention, difficulty managing behavior and inhibiting impulses, and hyperactivity (overactivity). The subtype names are used as descriptors based on which areas of functioning are affected.

Autism spectrum disorders (ASDs)—A group of disorders that in the past has included diagnoses of Autism, Asperger syndrome, and Pervasive Developmental Disorder Not Otherwise Specified (PDD-NOS) and are now all referred to as ASDs. Individuals with these disorders demonstrate weaknesses in social interaction and verbal and nonverbal communication and often show restrictive repetitive behaviors or interests. Each of these symptoms can run the gamut from mild to severe and appear differently in each individual. Hence, it's often said that "if you've met one person with autism, you've met one person with autism." In the late 1980s, autism activist Judy Singer, advocating that autism is a form of the neurodiversity that is present in all humans, coined the term *neurodiversity*. Journalist Harvey Blume made the term popular in the late 1990s when he wrote, "Neurodiversity may be every bit as crucial for the human race as biodiversity is for life in general. Who can say what form of wiring will prove best at any given moment? Cybernetics and computer culture, for example, may favor a somewhat autistic cast of mind." Though autism is one rendering of neurodiversity, the word itself truly signifies a biological characteristic seen in all human beings. Therefore, instead of this term's implying a disorder or an abnormality, we can begin to see it more broadly as encompassing all forms of human differences.

Cerebral palsy (CP)—A group of permanent movement disorders appearing in early childhood, caused by abnormal development or damage to the parts of the brain that control movement, balance, and posture. Symptoms often include poor coordination, stiff muscles, weak muscles, and tremors. There may also be problems with sensation, vision, hearing, swallowing, and speaking. Other symptoms may include seizures and difficulty with thinking or reasoning.

Down syndrome—A genetic disorder caused by the presence of all or part of a third copy of chromosome 21. Down syndrome is typically associated with physical growth delays, characteristic facial features, and mild to moderate intellectual disability. Individuals with Down syndrome often have better language understanding than ability to speak.

Intellectual disability—The American Association on Intellectual and Developmental Disabilities (AAIDD) defines intellectual disability as "significant limitations in both intellectual functioning (reasoning, learning, problem solving) and adaptive behavior, which covers a range of everyday social and practical skills." A third major criterion for this diagnosis is that onset of the above limitations is evident before the age of eighteen. Individuals who have intellectual disabilities most likely would have received a diagnosis of mental retardation in years past. Intellectual disabilities relate to one's cognitive or thought-processing abilities and fall under the umbrella term of developmental disabilities. The AAIDD states, "Developmental disabilities are severe chronic disabilities that can be cognitive or physical or both. The disabilities appear before the age of 22 and are likely to be lifelong. Some developmental disabilities are largely physical issues, such as cerebral palsy or epilepsy. Some individuals may have a condition that includes a physical and intellectual disability, for example Down syndrome or fetal alcohol syndrome."

Learning disabilities—A group of disorders that impact the academic achievement of individuals, regardless of their intellect. Individuals with dyslexia have difficulty processing the information they see when reading. Often a person with dyslexia will have trouble connecting the sound made by a specific letter to that letter or deciphering the sounds of all the letters together that form a word. Given these challenges, people with dyslexia often also have difficulty with writing, spelling, speaking, and math. Dysgraphia affects a person's writing abilities. People with dysgraphia may have a variety of weaknesses, including poor handwriting, difficulty with spelling, and difficulty putting thoughts down on paper. Though students with learning disabilities such as dysgraphia and dyslexia may have difficulty with conventional ways of teaching, they do have the ability to learn in a different manner.

Mood disorders—A group of disorders in which mood regulation deviates substantially from the norm and affects a person's ability to function. These include bipolar disorder and major depression. Depression typically involves a constant sense of hopelessness and despair. It may also include a loss of interest in normal activities and relationships. Bipolar disorder characteristics include severe changes in mood, including manic and depressive episodes. These can lead to risky behavior, damaged relationships and careers, and even suicidal tendencies.

Schizophrenia—A disorder characterized by a breakdown in thought processes and by poor emotional responsiveness. Schizophrenia most commonly features auditory hallucinations, paranoid or bizarre delusions, and/or disorganized speech and thoughts.

Tourette's syndrome—A genetically determined disorder characterized by childhood onset and the presence of tics, defined as sudden, repetitive, non-rhythmic motor movements or vocalizations involving discrete muscle groups. Some common tics are eye blinking, coughing, throat clearing, sniffing, and facial movements. It does not adversely affect intelligence. Movies and television have typically portrayed a stereotype of individuals with Tourette's shouting out obscene or socially inappropriate comments (coprolalia). This characteristic occurs only in about 10% of people with Tourette's syndrome.

Additional Resources

How Inclusive Is Your Parish?

Rate the following:	Very Well	Well	Poorly	Very Poorly	Strategic Improvement Goals
Our parish considers the needs of persons with disabilities (e.g., large-print missals, assistive listening devices).					
Our parish offers wheelchair-friendly access (e.g., wide doorways, access to the sanctuary).					
Our parish provides accommodations for persons with disabilities (e.g., sign-language interpreters).					
Our parish offers catechesis that is inclusive of persons with disabilities (e.g., adaptive catechesis, sensory kits).					
Our parish includes families of children with disabilities (e.g., gift bearers, greeters).					
Our pastoral staff supports a disability-ministry program (e.g., awareness efforts, creative outreach).					
Our parish includes parishioners with disabilities in volunteer opportunities (e.g., ministry fairs, parish bazaars).					
Our parish responds to the needs of individuals with disabilities through sacramental preparation and celebration (e.g., low-gluten hosts, adaptive catechesis).					

The Adaptive Teacher ➡ Faith-Based Strategies to Reach and Teach Learners with Disabilities

Inclusive Learning Environment

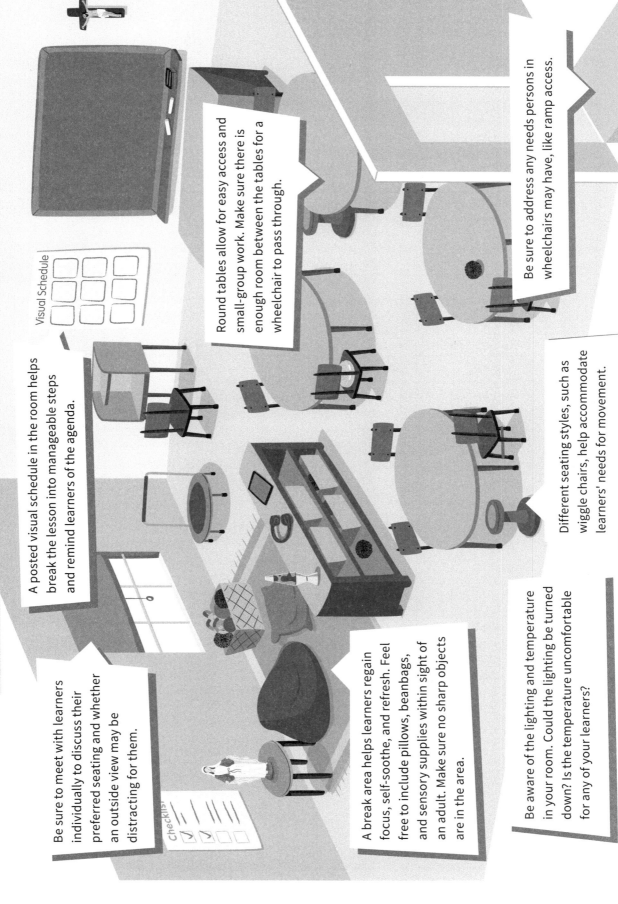

Visual Schedule

A posted visual schedule in the room helps break the lesson into manageable steps and remind learners of the agenda.

Round tables allow for easy access and small-group work. Make sure there is enough room between the tables for a wheelchair to pass through.

Be sure to address any needs persons in wheelchairs may have, like ramp access.

Different seating styles, such as wiggle chairs, help accommodate learners' needs for movement.

Be sure to meet with learners individually to discuss their preferred seating and whether an outside view may be distracting for them.

A break area helps learners regain focus, self-soothe, and refresh. Feel free to include pillows, beanbags, and sensory supplies within sight of an adult. Make sure no sharp objects are in the area.

Be aware of the lighting and temperature in your room. Could the lighting be turned down? Is the temperature uncomfortable for any of your learners?

Church Documents on Disabilities

Date	Document	Key Statement(s)
1978	*Pastoral Statement on Persons with Disabilities,* USCC	People with disabilities "seek to serve the community and to enjoy their full baptismal rights as members of the Church" (no. 33); and "The Church finds its true identity when it fully integrates itself with [persons with disabilities]" (no. 12).
1995	*Guidelines for the Celebration of the Sacraments with Persons with Disabilities,* USCCB	"By reason of their Baptism, all Catholics are equal in dignity in the sight of God, and have the same divine calling" (no. 1). Therefore, "Catholics with disabilities have a right to participate in the sacraments as full functioning members of the local ecclesial community" (no. 2).
1997	*General Directory for Catechesis,* USCCB	"Every Christian community considers those who suffer handicaps, physical or mental, as well as other forms of disability—especially children—as persons particularly beloved of the Lord.... Education in the faith, which involves the family above all else, calls for personalized and adequate programs" (#189).
1998	*Welcome and Justice for Persons with Disabilities: A Framework of Access and Inclusion,* USCCB	"Catechetical programs should be accessible to persons with disabilities and open to their full, active and conscious participation, according to their capacity" (no. 5). Fellow Christians should "recognize and appreciate the contribution persons with disabilities can make to the Church's spiritual life, and encourage them to do the Lord's work in the world according to their God-given talents and capacity" (no. 7).
2005	*National Directory for Catechesis,* USCCB	The involvement of persons with disabilities "enriches every aspect of Church life. They are not just the recipients of catechesis—they are also its agents" (#49).
2011	*Life Matters: Persons with Disabilities,* USCCB Respect Life Program pamphlet	"In short, as persons with disabilities share their gifts and needs, they bring out the best in our mutual humanity. They challenge us to live the Gospel precepts of charity in the real world, to sacrifice some of our comfort for others, to take the time to enable them to be full members of society. They need to feel our solidarity with them, and to know their true dignity and worth as fellow sisters and brothers in Christ. Our own future with Christ depends on it."
2017	*Guidelines for the Celebration of the Sacraments with Persons with Disabilities,* Revised Edition, USCCB	"It is essential that all forms of the liturgy be completely accessible to persons with disabilities, since these forms are the essence of the spiritual tie that binds the Christian community together. To exclude members of the parish from these celebrations of the life of the Church, even by passive omission, is to deny the reality of that community. Accessibility involves far more than physical alterations to parish buildings. Realistic provision must be made for Catholics with disabilities to participate fully in the Eucharist and other liturgical celebrations."

Adapted from Donna Toliver Grimes, *All God's People: Effective Catechesis in a Diverse Church.* (Chicago: Loyola Press, 2017), reprinted with permission.

People-First Language Guide

People with disabilities are, first and foremost, *people*. Each person has unique abilities, interests, and needs. People with disabilities enliven and enrich our families, schools, parishes, and communities. The language that a parish or school community uses to refer to persons with disabilities shapes overall beliefs and ideas. When we use thoughtful language that emphasizes the person over the disability, we are using people-first language. People-first language is an objective way of acknowledging, communicating, and reporting information that can be used to help make decisions that best serve the person.

Use This Language	Instead of This Language
the person with disabilities	the handicapped person; the disabled person
the person without disabilities	the normal person; the healthy person; the whole person; the typical person
the person who has a congenital disability	the person with the birth defect
the person who has been diagnosed with	the victim of; the person who is afflicted with; the person who suffers from
the person who has Down syndrome	the Downs person; the mongoloid person
the person who has autism	the autistic person
the person with quadriplegia; the person with paraplegia; the person diagnosed with a physical disability	the quadriplegic; the paraplegic
the person with a physical disability	the cripple; the crippled person
the person of short stature; the little person	the dwarf; the midget
the person who is unable to speak; the person who uses a communication device	the dumb person; the mute person; the mute
the person who is blind; the person who has a visual impairment	the blind person
the person with a learning disability	the learning-disabled person
the person diagnosed with a cognitive disability; the person with an intellectual and developmental disability	the mentally retarded person; the retard; the slow person; the idiot; the moron
the person who receives special-education services	the special ed/special-education student
the person who uses a wheelchair or a mobility chair	the person confined to a wheelchair; the wheelchair-bound person
accessible parking, bathrooms, and so on	handicapped parking, bathrooms, and so on

Adapted from *Adaptive Finding God Program Catechist Guide* (Chicago: Loyola Press, 2016), www.loyolapress.com.

Getting to Know Me Worksheet

Name _____

Nickname _____

Birthday _____

Interests

What do you like to do in your free time? _____

What is one special talent that you have? _____

What subject or topic do you know the most about? _____

Do you like to sing or dance or play an instrument? _____

Favorites

What are your favorite foods? _____

What are your favorite hobbies or activities? _____

What is your favorite color? _____

People

What do you love about your family? _____

Whom do you like to spend time with when you're not in school? _____

When you're planning or practicing something, do you like to work in groups,
with a partner, or alone? _____

Faith

Do you have a favorite prayer? ☐ Yes ☐ No   If so, which one? _____

What do you want to learn about your faith? _____

What part of God's creation makes you really happy? _____

Where do you like to go when you want to feel God's peace? _____

Do you like to sing songs about your faith? ☐ Yes ☐ No

Excerpted from *Adaptive Finding God Program Catechist Guide* (Chicago: Loyola Press, 2016), www.loyolapress.com.

Saints for People with Disabilities

Saint Ignatius of Loyola

Blessed Margaret of Castello: *A Blessed with Multiple Disabilities*

Blessed Margaret (1287–1320) was born with multiple disabilities, including blindness. Her aristocratic family abandoned her as a young child. Margaret would later go on to join the Third Order Dominicans.

Saint Pope John Paul II: *A Saint Who Had Parkinson's Disease*

Saint Pope John Paul II (1920–2005) modeled how to live with grace as he experienced the disabilities that come with age. He also showed us how to die with grace.

Saint Ignatius of Loyola: *A Saint with a Disability Caused by an Injury*

Saint Ignatius (1491–1556) was wounded by a cannonball during battle and forced into a long convalescence. During this period, he carefully examined his life and was inspired by the examples of the saints. Ignatius, who walked with a limp the rest of his life, would go on to found the Jesuits and build the framework for Ignatian spirituality.

Saint Kateri Tekakwitha: *A Saint with Physical Changes Resulting from a Disease*

Saint Kateri Tekakwitha (1656–1680), an Algonquin and Mohawk Native American, became seriously scarred and partially blinded from chicken pox at the age of four. Kateri grew to the highest levels of sanctity and faith in her tribe and became known as the Lily of the Mohawks. She was the first Native American to become a saint.

Saint Thérèse of Lisieux: *A Saint with a Terminal Illness*

Saint Thérèse of Lisieux (1873–1897) died of tuberculosis at the age of twenty-four. Known as "the Little Flower," Thérèse described in *Story of a Soul* how any person can attain the highest level of spirituality by living with love and paying attention to the life in front of them. She called this "the Little Way." Thérèse was the youngest and third female Doctor of the Church.

Saint Lucy: *A Martyr and Patron Saint of People with Blindness*

According to various accounts, Saint Lucy (283–304) had her eyes removed because of her steadfastness to God and her faith. While her full story is uncertain, she is the patron saint of blindness and eye disorders.

Saint Dymphna: *The Patron Saint of People with Mental Illness and Neurological Disorders*

Saint Dymphna was the daughter of an Irish king who had a mental illness. She fled to Belgium in the seventh century to escape his abuse. He later sent soldiers to kill the princess and her companions. Saint Dymphna is now the patron saint of anxiety, mental and emotional illness, and neurological disorders.

Saint Giles: *A Patron Saint of People with Disabilities*

Saint Giles lived a holy, hermit-like life in the woods of Spain in the Middle Ages. He was wounded by an arrow and sustained permanent injuries. He is invoked against cancer, sterility, mental illness, childhood fears, convulsions, and depression.

Saint René Goupil: *A Saint Who Was Deaf*

Saint René Goupil (1608–1642) was originally unable to become a Jesuit because of hearing loss. He later became a lay assistant to the missions in New France in North America. He was killed there because the natives thought he was disobedient; in reality, he was unable to hear orders.

Saint Thomas Aquinas: *A Saint with a Speech Disorder*

Theologian Thomas Aquinas (1225–1274) was a student at the University of Paris, where he was called the Dumb Ox because he was large and spoke slowly. We know him today as a Doctor of the Church and the patron saint of students and Catholic universities.

Participant Information Form

Participant's name: _____   Nickname: _____

Diagnoses/Disabilities: _____   Age: _____

Address: _____

School attending, if applicable: _____

Level of placement in school: _____

Primary language spoken at home: _____

Participant's preferred learning style: ☐ Auditory   ☐ Visual   ☐ Hands On

COMMUNICATION

Does the participant communicate verbally?   ☐ Yes   ☐ No

Does the participant use sign language/ASL?   ☐ Yes   ☐ No

Does the participant use an electronic device?   ☐ Yes   ☐ No

Strengths: _____

Needs, limitations, or restrictions: _____

MOVEMENT/MOBILITY

Strengths: _____

Needs, limitations, or restrictions: _____

SENSORY (vision, hearing, tactile, etc.)

Strengths: _____

Needs, limitations, or restrictions: _____

TYPES OF ACTIVITIES/SENSORY INPUT

Avoids the following: _____

Craves the following: _____

BEHAVIOR/SOCIAL

Strengths: _____

Needs, limitations, or restrictions: _____

EMOTIONAL

Signs of becoming agitated or unhappy are: _____

_____

Types of events/activities that may trigger upset are: _____

_____

What may help regain emotional balance is: _____

_____

SELF-HELP SKILLS (eating, using the restroom, handwashing, etc.)

Strengths: _____

Needs, limitations, or restrictions: _____

GENERAL HEALTH/MEDICAL

Strengths: _____

Needs, limitations, or restrictions: _____

If able to read, at what approximate grade level: _____

State approximate developmental level, in years: _____

Favorite interests, hobbies, activities: _____

List any incentives or rewards that are particularly effective: _____

_____

List any allergies: _____

Will have an EpiPen with him or her: ☐ Yes   ☐ No

List any food restrictions: _____

List any restrictions on activities: _____

Any history of seizures: ☐ Yes   ☐ No

If yes, type: _____   Frequency: _____

HISTORY OF SACRAMENTS RECEIVED

Date/location of the sacrament of Baptism: _____

_____

Date/location of the sacrament of Reconciliation: _____

_____

Date/location of the sacrament of First Holy Communion: _____

_____

Date/location of the sacrament of Confirmation: _____

_____

Primary Contact: _____

Relationship: _____

Cell phone: _____   E-mail: _____

Address (if different from participant): _____

Secondary Contact: _____

Relationship: _____

Cell phone: _____   E-mail: _____

Address (if different from primary): _____

Sensory Considerations Parent Questionnaire

Child's Name _____   Child's Age _____

Parent/guardian's name who is completing this questionnaire _____

May I call you for more information? ☐ Yes ☐ No   If yes, at what number? _____

SIGHT

How close or far away should your child be from me, the chalkboard or whiteboard, or displays? _____

Is your child affected by the lighting in a room? ☐ Yes ☐ No

If so, how? _____

Can decorations or displays be overstimulating or distracting? ☐ Yes ☐ No

If so, in what ways? _____

What does your child enjoy looking at? _____

_____

Does your child need visual cues or reminders, such as a visual schedule? ☐ Yes ☐ No

If so, what cues or reminders do you use? _____

HEARING

How close or far away should your child be from me in order to hear well? _____

Does your child become stressed with noise from other children or music? ☐ Yes ☐ No

If so, what noises? _____

What white noises, if any, does your child find soothing? _____

SMELL

Do certain materials, such as modeling clay, have smells that cause stress or anxiety? ☐ Yes ☐ No

If so, which ones? _____

Do certain rooms have smells that cause stress? ☐ Yes ☐ No

If so, which rooms? _____

What scents, if any, does the child find pleasing? _____

TASTE

What foods should be avoided because of allergies or dietary restrictions? _____

_____

_____

Do certain food textures or tastes cause your child stress or anxiety?　☐ Yes　☐ No

If so, which ones? _____

TOUCH

Which textures might be unpleasant for your child to touch? _____

Are certain textures soothing?　☐ Yes　☐ No

    If so, which ones? _____

Is your child drawn to certain textures that should not be used?　☐ Yes　☐ No

    If so, which ones? _____

Does your child have difficulty understanding when or how to touch things or people?　☐ Yes　☐ No

    If so, under what circumstances? _____

Does your child like to feel air circulating, or does he or she like to work in a room that is still? _____

TEMPERATURE

Is your child fidgety or lethargic if the room is too cold or too warm? _____

What is the ideal temperature for the room? _____

SENSE OF BALANCE

What gross-motor activities should be avoided because of your child's sense of balance? Please explain.

_____

_____

What gross-motor activities does your child like that help him or her learn?

_____

_____

BODY AND LIMB AWARENESS IN SPACE

What gestures or movements might be difficult for your child to perform?

_____

_____

What gestures or movements might cause your child to feel self-conscious or embarrassed?

_____

_____

_____

What activities or games include gestures or movements that might be fun for your child or build his or her self-esteem?

_____

_____

_____

PAIN TOLERANCE

How sensitive is your child to pain? What activities should I avoid that might be physically painful to him or her that may not be readily apparent?

_____

_____

_____

If your child doesn't react to seemingly painful circumstances, how can I protect him or her from harm?

_____

_____

_____

SENSE OF TIME

What activities might cause your child to lose track of time or lose the point of the lesson by becoming overly engrossed?

_____

_____

_____

What activities does your child really enjoy and spend quality time doing?

_____

_____

_____

Adapted from *Adaptive Finding God Program Catechist Guide* (Chicago: Loyola Press, 2016), www.loyolapress.com.

I Can Pause Before Answering

When you want to participate: check three boxes, and then raise your hand.

✓	✓	✓

Visual Feelings Dictionary

Afraid

Angry

Confident

Excited

Happy

Nervous

Sad

Shy

Silly

Sleepy

Surprised

Upset

The Adaptive Teacher ➡ Faith-Based Strategies to Reach and Teach Learners with Disabilities

Visual Schedule

A visual schedule is a management tool that shows a learner what activities will occur and in what sequence. Visual schedules help set expectations, help a learner remain organized, lessen stress, and can serve as powerful motivators. Visual schedules should be individualized and be of a size and format that they can accompany the learner as he or she moves from activity to activity. A visual schedule should show time progression vertically or horizontally from the first to the last activity. A visual representation or symbol should appear for each activity or time block on the schedule. You can use photographs, realistic drawings, icons, or small objects to represent each block.

Here is one example of how to make a visual schedule.

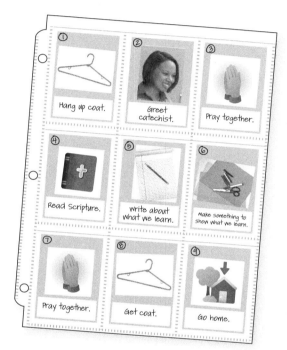

What You Need

▶ three-ring binder

▶ transparent three-ring binder insert for collecting cards

▶ note cards, cut into individual pieces that will slide into each sleeve of the insert

▶ small photographs or picture icons to represent the general activities that the child will participate in during faith formation

▶ glue

In Advance

Gather small photographs or picture icons to represent the general activities that the learner will participate in during faith formation, such as hang up coat (hanger), greet catechist (photo of catechist), pray (folded hands), read Scripture (Bible), write about what we learn (pencil and paper), make something to show what we learn (scissors, construction paper, crayons), pray (folded hands), get coat (hanger), go home (photo of parent or house).

Mount each photo or picture on a note card that has been cut to slide into the three-ring binder insert for collecting cards.

Prepare the Learner

Before class, assemble the schedule by inserting each note card into the sleeve in order from first to last. When the learner arrives, introduce the schedule and talk about each activity block. Then begin your lesson. As the learner completes each activity on the schedule, congratulate him or her, and if the learner likes it, turn over the note card to show that the activity is complete.

Increasing Ownership

Encourage independence and ownership by transferring teacher initiation and operation of the schedule to the learner, with the ultimate goal of the learner building and tracking his or her own schedule each session.

Adapted from *Adaptive Finding God Program Catechist Guide* (Chicago: Loyola Press, 2016), www.loyolapress.com.

Recommended Resources

BOOKS AND TOOLS

A Place for All: Ministry for Youth with Special Needs by John E. Barone (Winona, MN: Saint Mary's Press, 2008).

Adaptive Confirmation Preparation Kit for Individuals with Autism and Other Special Needs (Chicago: Loyola Press, 2014). www.loyolapress.com (Also available in Spanish).

Adaptive Finding God Program (Chicago: Loyola Press, 2016). www.loyolapress.com.

Adaptive First Eucharist Preparation Kit for Individuals with Autism and Other Special Needs (Chicago: Loyola Press, 2012). www.loyolapress.com (Also available in Spanish).

Adaptive Reconciliation Kit for Individuals with Autism and Other Special Needs (Chicago: Loyola Press, 2012). www.loyolapress.com (Also available in Spanish).

Faith, Family, and Children with Special Needs: How Catholic Parents and Their Kids with Special Needs Can Develop a Richer Spiritual Life by David Rizzo *(Chicago: Loyola Press, 2012).*

Finding God: Our Response to God's Gifts, Catechist Guide (Chicago: Loyola Press, 2016).

Guidelines for the Celebration of the Sacraments with Persons with Disabilities (Washington, DC: United States Conference of Catholic Bishops, 1995, Rev. 2017). www.usccb.org.

How to Talk to Children about People with Disabilities by Charleen Katra (New London, CT: Twenty-Third Publications, 2019).

How to Welcome, Include, and Catechize Children with Autism and Other Special Needs: A Parish-Based Approach by Lawrence R. Sutton, Ph.D. (Chicago: Loyola Press, 2013).

Jesus the Teacher, plush figure with *A Child's Bible,* www.loyolapress.com/learningtools.

My Picture Missal Flip Book and App, www.loyolapress.com/learningtools.

Pastoral Statement of U.S. Catholic Bishops on Persons with Disabilities (Washington, DC: United States Catholic Conference, Inc., 1978). www.usccb.org.

Praying the Rosary Concept Kit (Chicago: Loyola Press, 2015), www.loyolapress.com/learningtools.

Salt and Light: Church, Disability, and the Blessing of Welcome for All by Maureen Pratt (New London, CT: Twenty-Third Publications, 2018). www.twentythirdpublications.com.

Welcome and Justice for Persons with Disabilities (Washington, DC: United States Conference of Catholic Bishops, 1998). www.usccb.org.

ONLINE RESOURCES

3-Minute Retreat,
https://www.loyolapress.com/our-catholic-faith/prayer/3-minute-retreats

Archdiocese of Galveston-Houston's Ministry with Persons with Disabilities page,
https://tinyurl.com/y8xeboew

Archdiocese of Washington's Ministry for Persons with Disabilities,
https://adw.org/living-the-faith/special-needs/ministry-persons-disabilities/

Archdiocese of Washington's Deaf Ministries,
https://adw.org/living-the-faith/special-needs/deaf-ministries/

Autism Society, http://www.autism-society.org/

Catholic Celiac Society, http://www.ncpd.org/node/465

Catholic Coalition for Special Education, http://www.ccse-maryland.org/

Deaf Apostolate of the Archdiocese of Philadelphia's app to teach young children how to
pray in American Sign Language, www.religiousaslapp.org/

Loyola Press's Special needs resources,
www.loyolapress.com/our-catholic-faith/parish-ministry/special-needs

National Alliance on Mental Illness, https://www.nami.org/

National Catholic Education Association, (NCEA), https://www.ncea.org/. See also NCEA's
Exceptional Learner Resources page, https://tinyurl.com/yyxbm2lo

National Catholic Office for the Deaf, http://www.ncod.org/

National Catholic Partnership on Disability, (NCPD), www.ncpd.org/

National Catholic Partnership on Disability, (NCPD): Council on Intellectual Developmental
Disability, www.ncpd.org/about/councils/CIDD

National Catholic Partnership on Disability, (NCPD): Council on Mental Illness,
www.ncpd.org/ministries-programs/micouncil/catechesis/suicide

National Down Syndrome Society, (NDSS), https://www.ndss.org/

Pathways.org Inclusion in Worship,
https://pathways.org/tools-resources/inclusion-worship/

United Cerebral Palsy, https://ucp.org/

University of Dayton Institute for Pastoral Initiatives,
https://udayton.edu/artssciences/ctr/ipi/index.php

University of Dayton Virtual Learning Community for Faith Formation's Certificate in
Special Needs, https://vlcff.udayton.edu/certificates/special_needs.php

Xavier Society for the Blind, http://www.xaviersocietyfortheblind.org/

Note: For additional Catholic Disability Ministry information, training and resources, please
search local and national (arch)diocesan websites. Or search "Catholic Disability (or
Inclusion) Ministry"